# Live It Up Without Outliving Your Money!
## Revised and Updated Edition

# Live It Up Without Outliving Your Money!

## GETTING THE MOST FROM YOUR INVESTMENTS IN RETIREMENT

### Revised and Updated Edition

### Paul Merriman

**WILEY**

John Wiley & Sons, Inc.

Published by John Wiley & Sons, Inc., Hoboken, New Jersey.
Published simultaneously in Canada.

For general information on our other products and services or for technical support, please contact our Customer Care Department within the United States at (800) 762-2974, outside the United States at (317) 572-3993 or fax (317) 572-4002.

Wiley also publishes its books in a variety of electronic formats. Some content that appears in print may not be available in electronic books. For more information about Wiley products, visit our web site at www.wiley.com.

*Library of Congress Cataloging-in-Publication Data:*

Merriman, Paul A., 1943 –
   Live it up without outliving your money! : getting the most from your investments in retirement / Paul Merriman.—1st ed.
      p.   cm.
   Includes index.
   ISBN 978-0-470-22650-6 (cloth)
      1. Finance, Personal.   2. Investments.   3. Financial security.   4. Retirement income—Planning.   I. Title.   II. Title: 10 steps to a perfect retirement portfolio. III. Title: Ten steps to a perfect retirement portfolio.
HG179.M432   2008
332.024'014—dc22
                                                              2008006122

Printed in the United States of America

10  9  8  7  6  5  4  3  2  1

# Contents

# Acknowledgments

*No duty is more urgent than giving thanks.*

—St. Ambrose

I could not have written this book—and I could not do the work that I do—without the fabulous support I receive from many people who have generously given their time, talent, wisdom, and encouragement. I have the good fortune to have wonderful close working partnerships with several very talented people.

Tom Cock Jr. helps me reach hundreds of thousands of readers and listeners. He is my co-host on *Sound Investing,* our weekly radio show, and creator of SoundInvesting.com, where those broadcasts are available online. Tom, former host of the weekly PBS series *Serious Money,* also is my partner in designing and leading our educational workshops.

I could write a whole chapter on the many ways my life is enriched by my son, Jeff Merriman-Cohen. Jeff is my boss, as chief executive officer of our company, freeing me to concentrate on what I do best. Jeff is a superb financial adviser, an excellent manager, and a pleasure to work with in every way. Perhaps best of all (and very rare), my son is a full partner and a true friend. Every father should be so lucky!

Every part of this book reflects the writing skills of Richard Buck, managing editor of FundAdvice.com. Rich spent 20 years as a *Seattle Times* business reporter, and all that experience shows. Rich and I have great fun together generating and developing articles. Since

1993 he has been transforming my ideas into interesting, easy reading that has helped thousands of investors.

I am greatly indebted also to Dennis Tilley, who for many years was director of my company's research department. Dennis is literally a former rocket scientist who combines an amazing skill set with a passion for finding ways to improve investor returns. His work is woven throughout this book. Larry Katz, our very talented director of research, produced most of the updated tables in this book. Hang Nguyen, the third member of our research department, created an extremely important part of the book, our suggested fund portfolios.

Over the years, many people have helped me get my message out to investors. I am indebted to Craig Tolliver, who invited me to write a weekly column at CBSMarketWatch.com (now DowJonesMarketWatch.com); to Ken and Daria Dolan, who invited me to be a guest on their nationally syndicated radio and television shows; to Paul Kangas of *Nightly Business Report;* Humberto Cruz, a syndicated newspaper columnist; and Paul Farrell, a writer at DowJonesMarketWatch who shares my commitment to helping investors distinguish between what I call "investment pornography" and legitimate advice.

Bill Donoghue introduced me to thousands of investors at his Donoghue Mutual Fund Superstars conferences; Kim and Charles Githler of Intershow did the same with their wonderful Money Shows across the country. Wayne Baxmann of the American Association of Individual Investors has made it possible for me to speak at dozens of AAII chapters.

From Dan Wheeler, Bo Cornell, Eugene Fama, and Kenneth French I have learned the power of putting together world-class investments using what I believe are the best mutual funds on the planet. Every reader who follows my advice in Chapters 6 through 10 is also indebted to these individuals.

Finally, I must mention two very special people in my life: Thaddeus Spratlen and Dr. Lynn Staheli. They have inspired me to realize that I don't ever want to retire, because I'm simply having too much fun and there's too much still to be done.

Thaddeus, professor emeritus at the University of Washington, was one of my teachers long ago and has been a friend for 40 years. He spent decades as a professor preparing students for successful careers. He's devoting his "retirement" years to the Business and Economic Development Program through which the University of

Washington Business School and Seattle Rotary put students and experienced business professionals together to help small businesses in Seattle's inner city.

Lynn, a retired physician from Children's Hospital in Seattle, started Global-HELP (global-help.org), a nonpolitical, humanitarian agency that distributes free publications to medical professionals in developing countries. I'm proud to be a founding member of this organization's board.

My highest aspiration in life is to be like Thaddeus and Lynn.

# Introduction

## WHY I WROTE THIS BOOK

*I am not a teacher but an awakener.*

—Robert Frost

This book is designed in part to help investors protect themselves from Wall Street practices that I saw firsthand many years ago. Fresh out of college in the 1960s, I became a broker for a large Wall Street firm. Training classes in New York quickly taught me the priorities that should dominate my working day.

I guess I was naive and too idealistic for Wall Street. I had looked forward to helping people with their money. It didn't take long to learn that Wall Street had only one high-priority objective: sell.

Sales, of course, required trading activity. Gradually, I realized Wall Street was infected with an attitude that didn't seem right to me: If the clients were content, they weren't doing the firm any good. No matter what the clients had done, it was the broker's job to persuade them to do something else.

Ideally, that "something else" involved buying proprietary products on which the big brokerage houses earned unusually high commissions. Sometimes brokers were offered incentives such as free trips. In most cases, the commissions and the cost of the trips were built into the price of the products. This allowed brokers to tell clients they could buy these products without paying any commission. The clients thought they were getting a special deal. We knew otherwise: They were being exploited.

I'll admit the sophisticated world of New York City held quite an allure to a young man from Wenatchee, Washington. Wall Street made the job fun, and it seemed as if there was lots of money to be made easily. But it didn't take me long to grow weary of a job that, I came to realize, was designed essentially to separate people from their money with little thought given to whether these people were getting something valuable in return.

Before long, I left the brokerage industry to follow other business pursuits that brought me much more satisfaction. This eventually also gave me enough financial success that I could open my own investment business and begin managing money for individuals in 1983. I vowed at the time to keep my business free from all conflicts of interest, and independence has allowed me to fulfill that pledge.

In working with thousands of investors since then, I have seen the unfortunate results of what happens when people do what Wall Street tells them to do.

- Millions of people who wouldn't leave on a vacation without a road map nevertheless set aside hundreds of thousands of dollars for retirement without knowing their destination or having any plan to get there.
- Investors leave the bulk of their money in popular but lazy investments that don't historically compensate them for the risks they entail.
- Investors don't understand the effects of expenses and taxes. As a result, they let far too much of their hard-won savings leak away.
- Investors make far-reaching decisions based on whims, emotions, or superficial tips from amateurs, salespeople, and advisers whose financial interests are in conflict with those of their clients.
- In the end, too many investors wind up with too little money and too much emotional stress.

My professional life is dedicated to teaching people how to take care of themselves and their families so they won't wind up with those unfortunate outcomes. Much of this teaching takes place in retirement workshops I lead every year. Tens of thousands of investors have found these sessions helpful and stimulating, and I thoroughly enjoy doing them. This book contains the most important material from those workshops.

In doing this work over the years, I've met a lot of great people (along with a few I'd be happy to forget), and I've had a lot of fun. I hope you will find some fun in these pages, too. I hope you'll find the book easy and enjoyable to read, something you'll want to share with somebody else.

Three serious objectives shaped this work: to educate, to stimulate, and to motivate.

Education is essential because there's simply too much data and information available to investors. Much of it is important, but much of it is a combination of noise and sales pitches. I've spent tens of thousands of hours identifying what matters to investors and what doesn't. In these pages you will learn which is which.

Stimulation is valuable because it gets people to think. If you go through this book chapter by chapter, I guarantee that you will think in new ways about investing, about psychology, about your money, and about your future.

Motivation is the most important goal, and at the same time the most elusive. If I have only convinced you that there is a better way, yet my words haven't persuaded you to take some action, then I have failed to motivate you. What you do or don't do, of course, is outside my control, as it should be. I don't know how to directly motivate you except to use words to paint pictures of what is possible and how your life could be. You'll find two direct examples of this in Chapter 2.

If at the end of this book you understand investing in ways that are brand-new to you, then I've done my job of education. If you can see the world around you in new ways and think about what you see in new ways, and if some of the stories from this book help you to notice things that you didn't notice before, then I have done my job of stimulation. And if you take action to improve the way you put your financial resources to work for you, then I have done my job of motivation.

If these things happen, then the many hours spent writing this book will have been worthwhile for me. I'm confident that the time you spend with this material will be no less worthwhile for you.

## Ten Steps to an Ideal Retirement Portfolio

Some people organize their thoughts best with a step-by-step list. This book isn't organized along those lines, but your mind may work best if it's following a list. So right here I'll give you my list of 10 steps to creating the retirement portfolio that's ideal for you. And I'll tell you where in the book to find out about each one.

This list may seem daunting, filled with tasks that would take you months or even years to complete. But here is something I've learned from leading workshops for people who are looking ahead to retirement: Most of these people can accomplish all 10 of these steps by attending a workshop and then spending 90 minutes with a professional adviser. This book gives you what's in my workshop. If you can manage another 90 minutes with a good adviser (plus the time it takes to do the necessary homework), you'll have all this done.

1. *Determine how much you will need to live on in retirement.* This will tell you how big your portfolio must be when you retire. And that in turn will tell you how much you need to save and what investment return you need. Chapter 5 tells you how to establish your basic target for the income you'll need from your portfolio. Most investors give this step too little attention. Investors who don't have this information are too often captivated by fear and greed, taking either too much risk or too little risk, depending on what's happening in the markets. This first step is necessarily the foundation for everything that follows.

2. *Determine how much you* want *to live on in retirement.* In Chapter 5, you'll find out how to establish your live-it-up retirement income target. This gives you a second figure for the target size of your portfolio and the return necessary to achieve it. We talk to many people who, having neglected to take this step, have invested as if they must achieve the highest possible return regardless of risk. Often, analysis will show that they can achieve all their goals with much less risk than they thought.

3. *Determine your tolerance for taking risks.* You'll find important insights on this topic throughout the book. Chapter 10 focuses on risk. For every investment you make, you

should understand the inherent risks involved and how this investment will affect the overall risk of your portfolio.

4. *Make all your decisions based on what's probable, not what's possible.* From 1995 through 1999, the Standard & Poor's 500 Index compounded at a rate of 28.5 percent a year, leading many people (including plenty who should have known better) to conclude that successful investing was easy. Some investors scoffed at me in 1999 when I refused to give serious consideration to questions like "What's a fund I can count on to make 75 percent a year?" I was dismissed as hopelessly old-fashioned when I suggested investors should aspire to long-term annual growth of 12 percent.

   The brief bull market bubble in 1999 showed us that returns of 75 percent were possible. But the bear market of 2000–2003 showed us that 75 percent losses were equally possible. As it turns out, we have more than three quarters of a century of history to show us what's probable. This, not the flash-in-the-pan excitement of a bull market, should be the basis for your planning.

5. *Determine the kinds of assets that will give you the returns you need to achieve your goals.* Academics have done years of mind-numbing research on this very topic—and some have even won Nobel Prizes for it. I have distilled that research into five chapters (6 through 10) that tell you what you need to know and what you should do about it. Actually, I think you may find this is quite interesting material. You'll learn how to add nine equity asset classes to the S&P 500 Index in order to achieve extra return without taking any more risk than that of this popular index.

6. *Combine those assets in the right proportions into a portfolio that's tailored specifically for you.* I show you exactly how to do that in Chapter 12. I name names of the specific funds you should use at Fidelity, Vanguard, T. Rowe Price, and other sources.

7. *Learn to recognize and control the expenses of investing.* Chapter 11 tells you how to recognize expenses as leaks in your portfolio and how to plug them. There are many things about investing that you can't control, but this is one that you can. Savvy investors pay lots of attention to expenses. Sloppy investors would rather not be bothered. Over a lifetime, the difference can add up to hundreds of thousands of extra dollars.

8. *Make sure you understand enough about the tax laws to avoid giving Uncle Sam more of your money than you are obligated to.* Lots of investors carelessly squander part of their assets because they don't pay attention to tax issues. This is a big topic, but we hit the high spots in Chapter 11. The advice you'll find there will help you turn your investments into an efficient machine that works as hard as possible for *you*, not for the tax man.

9. *Establish the right distribution plan that will give you the income you need in retirement along with the peace of mind of knowing you won't run out of money.* Of all the 10 steps, this one is taught and discussed the least when professionals and authors try to help people handle their money. Investors who bungle this by withdrawing too much too fast can wind up impoverished or broke in their old age. Investors at the other extreme can, sometimes without realizing it, pass up fantastic opportunities to enjoy life and contribute to others during their lifetimes. Chapter 13 tells you how to get this step right and gives you much to think about.

10. *Put everything you do on automatic pilot.* In more than 40 years of working with people and their money, I've seen again and again the value of making careful, thoughtful decisions and forming those decisions into a plan that can be executed automatically. Investors who do this are likely to achieve the highest returns among their peers at whatever level of risk is appropriate for them.

There are many good ways to accomplish this last step. Accumulate savings through dollar cost averaging. Invest in funds through automatic investment plans that take money out of your bank account regularly or through payroll deduction. Set up your portfolio for automatic rebalancing at the same time every year, using your electronic calendar to remind you if necessary. Fund your IRA in the first week of every year. If you can, do the same with your 401(k) or similar plan at work.

Invest in index funds, which by nature will automatically correct for the unexpected disasters in the market. If a big company goes into the tank unexpectedly (think of Enron or Bear Stearns), the S&P 500 Index will automatically correct for that with no action required from you. Set up your withdrawals automatically too, so you never have to worry about how much to take out or when.

In summary, organize your finances so that instead of taking up your time they simply support you while you do what makes your life worth living.

If you want what my schoolteachers used to call "extra credit," here's an 11th step: *Very carefully, choose and hire a financial adviser.* This is such a valuable move that I've devoted Chapter 14 to it.

If you apply yourself seriously to these 10 steps (and taking the 11th will make the others much easier and more likely to be successful), you will have the best possible chance for that ideal retirement.

## A Note to the Reader

Even a casual reader is likely to notice quickly that this book is unusual. This reflects the fact that not everybody learns the same way. It also reflects my personal commitment to make the material in this book as useful as possible and to keep it up to date for you, the reader.

This book is designed to be read at three levels. The simplest level makes it about a 30-page book. Every chapter begins with a brief introductory essay that presents the main points in the chapter, without the supporting evidence or a full discussion. If you want a general overview of what's in this book, you can get it by reading only those essays. Of course, I hope you will want to know more and will take the time to delve into the contents.

The second level is the main text, including graphs, charts, and tables. This is the heart of the book, the stuff that makes it worth your money and your time. The concepts presented here are not complex. If you enjoy reading the business sections of daily newspapers, you should have no trouble following my arguments and the evidence that backs them up.

Along the way you will see some graphs and tables unlike any that you're likely to be familiar with. If you have a little patience, understanding these illustrations won't be hard. They will help you to see information in new ways so that the important points become obvious at a glance.

You'll find the third level throughout the book in the form of highlighted text boxes that act as sidebars to illuminate ideas you might want to come back to for reference. You can skip these boxes without missing the main points of the book. But I hope you'll find them worth your while.

Inevitably, the numbers and the specific fund recommendations in this book will become outdated. The good news is that you'll always be able to find our current recommendations, along with updated versions of many of the tables in this book, online. You'll find this at my company's educational web site, FundAdvice.com. Be sure to visit this site for any updates to our suggested portfolios before you invest.

Finally, the Appendixes at the end of the book contain my suggestions for further reading and education.

Here's a final important note. I am the founder of a company in Seattle that provides investment education, advice, and management. We are in the business of managing money for clients.

My many years as a hands-on money manager have given me an enormous amount of practical experience with real people in real situations. This book is filled with stories and insights based on decades of being in the trenches, helping investors who, in many ways, may be like you.

Our business is carefully organized so that we have no conflict of interest with our clients. I have done my best to avoid anything self-serving in this book, and I have asked my editors to hold my feet to the fire in that regard. Still, I definitely have a point of view and some strong beliefs about what serves investors best. I am happy to let you be the final judge. Don't take what I say on blind faith. If you find my views credible, then please use them however you wish.

# CHAPTER 1

# Why Investors Fail

*If you don't know where you're going, you might wind up somewhere else.*

—Yogi Berra

Investing isn't terribly difficult, but it's a specialized area that requires careful navigation. A huge industry has evolved to use a multitude of clever ways to separate people from part of their retirement savings without necessarily providing much benefit in return. In simple terms, this means that neither your broker nor any of the array of experts on Wall Street is necessarily your friend or even on your side.

Think of investing as a journey. You start at one place and head for another. If you want to drive from California to Michigan quickly and painlessly, there are relatively few choices that make sense. Most will probably draw heavily on the interstate highways. But imagine how hard it would be to plan such a trip if sales forces for several hundred competing highways were giving you tantalizing promises, saying they could get you there better and faster if you would just choose their routes.

Investing is a little bit like that: The best route may be efficient though boring. Yet along the way there are hundreds of distractions and opportunities to get you off the track. Most people have a tough time making good investment decisions. They don't have the necessary training or the knowledge. The difficulty of understanding all the options sometimes appears greater than the benefits of doing so. As a result, somewhere along the way almost every investor makes at least one serious mistake. Some never seem to stop making mistakes.

In this chapter we look at some of the more serious ways that typical investors work against their own interests. Investors procrastinate or remain passive when the circumstances call for action. They ignore the effects of taxes and expenses. They don't think about their long-term and short-term goals in a clear, organized way. They don't have a written plan for how to get from where they are to where they're going. (Think of it as a road map. If you leave it at home, it's no help.)

Most investors occasionally take way too much risk. Sometimes they don't take nearly as much risk as they should. Investors pay too much of their hard-earned savings to other people who are not necessarily on their side. Too many investors act as if they think smiling salespeople are their friends. They put too much faith in institutions, as if they believe big companies are organized for their customers' benefit. They put too much faith in what they see on financial television, what they hear on the radio, and what they read in financial publications. In doing this, they fail to distinguish between facts (which can be very useful) and interpretation, persuasion, and marketing.

Without getting any particular benefit in return, too many investors give up liquidity, making it costly and inconvenient to get their money back when they need it. They have unrealistic expectations. They often treat investing as a competitive sport. They take investment advice or tips from strangers or amateurs. They invest in ways that fill their emotional needs instead of their financial ones. Thus, they give in to fear and greed, arguably the two most powerful forces on Wall Street. They put their money into investments they don't understand, leading to grief, loss, and disillusionment that sometimes prompt them to give up altogether.

Collectively, that's the bad news. Whew!

The good news is that investing does not have to be that hard. This book shows you precisely how to overcome all those hurdles and how to draw up a road map that's right for you. You'll learn how to implement that plan so that good investment decisions become automatic—instead of random events that seem to happen only by luck.

Investing is about taking risks. When you risk your capital, you are entitled to expect a fair return commensurate with the level of risk you take. But if you're not careful, your own mistakes can prevent you from achieving the return that should be yours.

When I meet with a new client, one of the first things we talk about is risk. It's a topic that most of the industry (and most investors) would be happy to avoid altogether. But investors who don't understand risk cannot understand the choices they must make as investors. You'll find numerous references to risks in this book, because it is a critical topic.

Imagine you are in a bank applying for a loan. Suddenly you realize that right at the next desk, Bill Gates is also applying for a loan. Who do you think the bank would rather lend money to? Bill, of course! Don't take it personally, but the bank would always rather lend its money to Bill than to you, because there is simply no question about his ability to pay the money back. He's as close to a risk-free, perfect borrower as the bank could wish for.

But it's not quite that simple. Bill Gates is not the sort of person who would hesitate to take advantage of his position. If he told the bank he wouldn't pay more than 5 percent interest, and if you were willing to pay 10 percent interest, what do you think the bank would do?

The bank can lend money to Bill and earn 5 percent in a risk-free transaction. Or it can lend money to you and collect twice as much. Obviously the bank would like the extra interest, but how reliable are you? Here's the rub, because the bank can't ever know for sure.

Therefore, the bank must decide if that extra return is worth the extra risk. And that is exactly the challenge that investors face. If you were the banker and you could make only one of those two loans, you'd have to tell your boss either "I turned down

Bill Gates for a loan," or "I turned down an opportunity to make twice as much money." Which one would you choose? Would you make that decision on your own without consulting your boss? Probably not!

In real life, bankers have the benefit of institutional and personal experience. They have policies and committees. They don't have to make decisions like that by the seat of their pants. But every day of every week, individual investors make exactly this type of decision without understanding the nature of what they are doing: taking risks that have real consequences.

I usually start my investing workshops by discussing a dozen or so common traps that investors get themselves into. Almost every investor makes at least a few of these mistakes, and I hope you won't feel there's anything wrong with you if some of them sound painfully familiar.

## Mistake 1: No Written Plan

According to every study I have seen, people with written plans for their investments wind up with much more money during retirement than those who don't have written plans.

This important document should spell out your main assumptions about inflation; future investment returns; how much you'll save before you retire; when you will retire; the amount of money you'll count on from fixed sources such as pensions, Social Security, and perhaps part-time employment; as well as the amount that you'll need to withdraw from your portfolio in retirement. Your written plan should specify how you will make asset allocation choices and where you'll get professional help when you need it.

By the time you finish this book, you'll know the most important things that should be in your written plan. And to give you more specific help, I suggest two excellent articles you'll find online at FundAdvice.com. One is called "Don't have an investment plan? Start here." The other is titled "Make success your policy."

## Mistake 2: Procrastination

If you wait for what you regard as the perfect time to get your investments organized or reorganized, the wait could ruin your results over a lifetime. Procrastination takes many forms. Some people don't start saving for retirement until it's nearly on top of them.

Other people know they should review their investments, yet they always give priority to other things.

Some investors are sure they will catch up later. The irony is that the longer they wait, the less time they have. And time, as anybody who has studied compound interest tables knows, is an investor's best friend. Once you know what you need to do, every day you delay is a day of opportunity that you can never get back.

## Mistake 3: Taking Too Much Risk

In the late 1990s, some relatively inexperienced investors began to act as if they believed investment risk had become only a theoretical concept. But the three-year bear market of 2000 through 2002 was a rude wake-up call. Some aggressive investors who were sure they knew what they were doing in 1999 found they had lost more than half their money within two years. I hope you won't let anything like that happen to you.

Most people understand, at least in general, that higher risks go along with higher returns. Yet too many investors act as if they are immune to risk. Or perhaps they believe they will somehow know when it's the right time to sell a risky investment they bought. Unfortunately, that realization rarely comes before there have been significant losses.

Investors typically don't make any up-front effort to understand the nature of the risks they are taking when they make an investment. Only rarely do they have a plan for what they will do if things don't turn out as expected. People who take too much risk often wind up being speculators rather than investors. Savvy investors, by contrast, pay a lot of attention to understanding, limiting, and managing the risks they take. If they speculate, they do so only with money they know they can afford to lose.

## Mistake 4: Taking Too Little Risk

Some people are paranoid about losing any money at all. They want things nailed down, secure, guaranteed. The majority of money in 401(k) plans, at least until the great bull market of the late 1990s, was invested in guaranteed interest contracts, bonds, money market funds, and similar low-risk securities. Those choices give investors the illusion of short-term security. But unfortunately, in the long run, it's only an illusion.

Especially after the bear market of 2000 to 2002, it may seem important to avoid losses. But an equally important risk, especially for young investors with many years ahead of them, is to give up the long-term gains they are likely to attain by investing in equities. Very-low-risk investments always come packaged with low returns. If your emergency money is in a bank account paying 2 percent interest, you may think there's no risk. But in fact, you are taking the very real risk (in the long term it's a virtual certainty) that inflation and taxes will rob your money of much of its purchasing power.

If you're saving for retirement 25 years down the road, and you opt for a very conservative mix of investments that is expected to return 7 percent annually instead of an all-equity portfolio with an expected annual return of 10 percent, you may be massively shortchanging yourself. After 25 years of contributions of $5,000 a year, a 7 percent portfolio will grow to $316,245. But invest the same amounts at 10 percent and you will have $491,735. (That difference, about $175,000, is much more than the total of all the 25 annual investments.)

## Mistake 5: Trusting Institutions

I often ask participants in my workshops if they trust their banks. Most of them answer with a pretty firm "*No!*" Yet most of us still habitually act as if we believe our banks will tell us if we should move our money in some way that would be more beneficial to us.

In fact, you and your bank have a classic conflict of interest. Your best interests are served by an account that pays the highest interest along with penalty-free access to your money whenever you need it. Your bank's best interests are served by accounts that pay you little or nothing. Your bank also wants you to buy products on which it can earn sales commissions, like load mutual funds and various types of insurance.

It's even worse than that. Perhaps the single most profitable thing that banks do is bounce checks on overdrawn accounts. Bankers who work in branches (and thus deal with customers face to face) will be happy to help you manage your money so that you don't bounce checks. But if every checking account customer were bounce-free for a year, billions of dollars in profits would vanish—and some executives in bank headquarters would find themselves looking for jobs.

Because of these conflicts, it's a mistake to rely on a bank to tell you what's in your best interest. The same is true of brokerage houses and insurance companies.

## Mistake 6: Believing the Media

The headlines on the covers of financial magazines are often predictable: "The Six Best New Funds"; "Found: The Next Microsoft"; "Everyone's Getting Rich—Here's How to Get Your Share." (Those are actual examples.) The purpose of those headlines is to get you to dive into the contents enough so you'll buy the magazine and see the advertising within. We discuss this in more detail in Chapter 4. Here are a couple of high points.

Serious investors need textbooks more than hot ideas. But most people would rather have entertainment, and that's what broadcast outlets and financial publications provide. Writers and editors and publications follow fads. They write about what's in favor and what's in style. When the winds of popularity change, you can bet that they won't be far behind. The purpose of these articles is not to help you. The purpose of the articles is to get you to buy the publications.

The right way to read financial articles that tout specific mutual funds and stocks is to treat those articles as entertainment. The wrong way is to regard them as prescriptions for investment decisions you should make. If you remember that, you might easily save yourself 1,000 times the cover price of this book.

## Mistake 7: Failing to Take Small Steps That Can Make Big Differences

Far too many people fail to make their IRA contributions at the start of the calendar year. Others fail to make IRA contributions at all. They leave money in taxable accounts instead of sheltering it in retirement accounts. They don't maximize their opportunities for corporate matching money in 40l(k) and similar plans. They have multiple small IRA accounts, paying annual fees for each one, instead of consolidating these assets into a single account that can avoid such fees and make rebalancing easier.

Bank customers, spurred by laziness or inertia or thinking that it doesn't matter, don't move their money from checking accounts into money market deposit accounts. Others don't move their money from money market deposit accounts to nonbank money market funds where they can earn more interest. Each of these steps seems small by itself, yet over a lifetime they can make a big difference—but only to people who act.

## Mistake 8: Buying Illiquid Financial Products

Liquidity is the ability to get your money back quickly without undue penalties. A stock is very liquid; you can turn it into cash whenever the market is open, and you'll have your cash in a few days. Mutual funds are even more liquid, letting you have your cash the following day if you have set up electronic transfers into a bank account. Money market funds and many bond funds give you same-day access to your money by letting you write a check.

But liquidity is severely compromised when you invest in limited partnerships, for which there is often no market. Liquidity is also impaired with variable annuities and shares in commissioned mutual funds that charge penalties for withdrawals made before certain waiting periods have expired.

Some people sink their rainy-day savings into their homes by making extra principal payments on their mortgages. But when that rainy day comes along, the only way to tap that extra principal may be to refinance (a time-consuming, expensive process) or sell the home. (And if you're facing financial troubles, your refinancing prospects could be at a low point.)

## Mistake 9: Requiring Perfection in Order to Be Satisfied

People who can't stand to have anything less than a perfect solution seldom make successful investors. No matter where you put your money, there will always be something that's performing better than what you have. And if you're lucky enough to own the one fund that's doing better than everything else, you can be certain it won't remain that way for long. That's just the nature of this business.

Perfectionists often flit from one thing to the next, chasing elusive performance. In real life, you get a premium for risk only if you stay the course. If you demand perfect investments, you won't ever stay with anything long enough for it to pay off.

## Mistake 10: Accepting Investment Advice and Referrals from Amateurs

If you had a serious illness, I hope you would consult a nurse or a doctor, not somebody on the street who happened to have an opinion on what you should do—or worse, somebody who had a product to sell you. I hope you treat your life savings and your financial future with the same care as you'd treat your health. Sad to say, too many people make financial decisions based on things they hear casually. The lure of the hot tip is all but irresistible to some investors. But as painful as it is, there are no safe shortcuts to wealth.

A client once told me he had heard about a woman who made a lot of money for some of his friends. My client, normally a very conservative man, cashed in $250,000 of his long-term investments and turned it over to this woman, who told him she would invest it in "a conservative strategy." Within two months, she had lost half his money. Only then did this client investigate enough to learn that the woman he had trusted was not even licensed to do what she was doing. Her compensation was to be 20 percent of whatever profits he made. That gave her an incentive to generate big profits quickly. Unfortunately for my client, he had assumed all the risks, giving her no incentive to avoid going for broke in hopes of making a big score. When her efforts failed, she could walk away, leaving him with the losses.

## Mistake 11: Letting Emotions Drive Investment Decisions

The two most powerful forces that drive decisions on Wall Street are emotional: fear and greed. Think about this the next time you listen to a radio or television commentator explaining what's happening in the stock market. You'll hear echoes of fear and greed over and over.

Some investors fear rising interest rates; others fear falling interest rates. Some fear inflation while others welcome it. You name it, somebody's afraid of it. Fear is why so many investors bail out of carefully planned investment strategies when things look bleak. Investors sell en masse when prices are down; that reduces profits and increases losses.

Greed, likewise, blinds investors and makes them forget what they should know. In the last half of 1999 and the first half of 2000, greed prompted many investors to stuff their portfolios with high-flying technology stocks. But in the spring of 2000, most of those stocks plunged without warning. This quickly transformed many greedy investors into fearful investors.

The desire to make money is legitimate. But unless it is tempered with a healthy respect for risk, it turns into greed. Likewise, the desire to avoid or limit losses is legitimate. But when it is allowed to run amok, it turns into fear.

## Mistake 12: Putting Too Much Faith in Short-Term Performance

Many investors, especially inexperienced ones, spend far too much time and energy trying to forecast what essentially cannot be forecast: short-term performance. Worse, they give far too much credence to recent short-term performance. We tend to think that whatever just happened will continue to happen. Sometimes that's true, but a lot of the movement in the stock market is essentially random. That's one reason recent performance is a lousy predictor of future performance.

## Mistake 13: Overconfidence

Many investors get into trouble when they start believing that they really know what they are doing. They become overconfident. There's an old saying on Wall Street to the effect that every 1 percent increase in a bull market makes investors think their IQs have gone up a point.

Many overconfident investors put too much of their money into a single stock or a single fund. Then they get emotionally attached, and their attachment takes on a life of its own. Investors' overconfidence tends to persist even when a favored investment starts heading downward. By the time such an investor is finally willing to admit that things have changed, he will probably have stayed much too long.

## Mistake 14: Focusing on the Wrong Things

We talk a lot in this book about asset allocation, the choice of what kind of assets go into your portfolio. It's generally accepted that asset allocation accounts for about 97 percent of investors' returns.

That leaves about 3 percent for choosing specific stocks and mutual funds—the very thing on which most investors spend almost all their time and energy.

Even when investors have properly allocated their portfolios, they can focus on the wrong things. This happens when they zero in on small parts of their portfolios instead of the whole package. They can become obsessed with a small investment that seems to stubbornly refuse to do its part during a bull market. In fact, it's normal and expected for investments to go down as well as up, even during a bull market. That's what makes it possible to *buy low,* an essential part of what may be the most fundamental rule in investing: buying low and selling high. But quite often I have encountered enraged investors who want to overthrow their entire portfolio because of what happens to some small part of it.

This wouldn't be such a problem if investors had a better understanding of diversification. A properly diversified portfolio will inevitably always include some investments that are lagging. This is fine, because whatever is performing well at any given time won't necessarily continue to do so. And when that happens, you want some other asset class waiting in the wings to have its day in the sun, so to speak.

## Mistake 15: Needing Proof before Making a Decision

This is a variation of two previously mentioned mistakes: procrastination and requiring perfection. The ultimate stalling tactic for investors who aren't ready to make a move is to require one more piece of information or evidence. You can get evidence for just about any view of the market you want, but you cannot get proof. You can prove what happened in the past, but there's no way to prove anything about the future. It has always struck me as ironic that the main focus of mutual fund advertising is past performance, yet that's the one thing that the funds can't sell and the very thing that investors can't buy.

If you must have certainty, stick to Treasury bills and certificates of deposit. If you're seeking returns higher than those give, you will have to accept some uncertainty. The only certain thing about the future is that it won't look just like the past. Savvy investors who understand that will hedge their bets by diversifying. Remember, investors get paid to take calculated risks. They can't do that if they must know in advance how things are going to turn out.

## Mistake 16: Not Knowing How to Deal with the First 15 Mistakes

The cures for all these mistakes may seem obvious, but they are not necessarily easy. They boil down to education, discipline, and managing your emotions. Throughout this book you will find hundreds of ways that should help you do just that. Here are a few thoughts right now, while all this investment carnage is fresh in your mind.

- Make sure you have a written investment plan—even if it's only on a single piece of paper—that outlines what you must do to achieve your long-term and short-term goals. Include specific measurable interim goals so you can keep track of your progress.
- Educate yourself. Finish this book and continue learning from the suggested reading list in the Appendix and from the online article library at www.FundAdvice.com.
- If you don't understand an investment, don't put your money into it. I believe this single step will prevent more grief than almost anything else you can do.
- Sometimes the best course may be simply to slow down. Take a deep breath and apply a liberal dose of patience. It's probably the most underrated virtue I know in this fast-paced world.
- Finally, if you notice that emotions are driving your decisions, substitute a discipline. If you have trouble finding or implementing a proper discipline, consider professional investment advice or money management.

In the end, the best prescription for avoiding most mistakes is summed up in just one word: *diversification*.

# 2

# Stress versus Success

## A TALE OF TWO INVESTORS

*Content makes poor men rich. Discontent makes rich men poor.*
—Benjamin Franklin

There's a big difference between people who get retirement right and those who get it wrong. This difference is a combination (in rough order of importance) of attitude, habits, mental clarity, discipline, diligence, determination, and a lifetime of cumulative choices. Oh, and good luck doesn't hurt—but don't rely on it.

Most of us make choices all the time that will help determine whether our retirement years are golden or gloomy. Whether you're planning your retirement in the future, you're on the verge of retiring or you're already retired, you will stack the odds in your favor if you learn what separates successful retirees from those who are doomed to struggle.

You might learn these things from reading lists of smart moves and dumb moves. But you're more likely to remember a picture of success contrasted with a picture of struggle. In this chapter I introduce you to two of my longtime clients, whom I'll call George and Roger.

George seems to have done everything right. Roger has done so many things wrong that I hate to think what his life must be like. I've changed their names and a few biographical details to protect these people's identities. Otherwise, the following stories are true and accurate.

## George: Doing It Right

If you could meet George Caldwell, a former Army officer and surgeon, I'm almost certain you would like him. The same goes for his wife, Ruth, an accomplished musician with a charming personality. After he left the service as a lieutenant colonel, George went into private practice for 14 years as a surgeon.

George and Ruth agreed that the first claim on their income every year would be to make the maximum allowed contribution to a tax-deferred retirement plan. "We saved first, and what we had left over was what we could live on," he said.

Even though they had more than enough for a comfortable life, George and Ruth made a point of living below their means. "My friends were driving Jaguars and Mercedes, but we didn't. We drove Hondas, and I still drive a used Honda. We didn't play big shots, because that wasn't important to us. We lived in a house that was very modest compared to everybody we knew." George and Ruth always shopped for the best deal on everything they bought, and they never felt deprived. Ruth can afford to drive any car she wants. Last time I checked in with her, she was driving an 11-year-old economy sedan.

While he was working, George dabbled at investments and once had a fairly complicated strategy that required him to watch the market every business day. Once when he was out of the country he left his paperwork at home and could not keep up with his systems. He lost more than $6,000. He remembers the lesson much more than the money he lost. He later consolidated all his accounts into a simpler strategy that has Ruth's blessing. Though she leaves investment decisions to him, "I run big decisions past her in advance because she has a lot of good sense," George says. "When we disagree on something, we work it out until we are both satisfied."

A frugal lifestyle and conservative investments mean they can live the life they want. She pursues music, he pursues travel and other interests. To fund a major three-month trip to Antarctica, George didn't raid the couple's retirement portfolio. Instead they simply cut back on other expenses for a while.

George's formula sounds easy: Make a bundle of money, save a lot of it, and keep your spending down. But doing this has required them to carefully, deliberately choose between what is important to them and what is not. They have set realistic investment goals. And they've managed to avoid the disagreements and power struggles that derail the financial plans of many couples.

I asked George what he would recommend to somebody who was about to retire. "I'd say you have to do some figuring. Look at what you have and what you'll need. Examine your lifestyle and what it will cost you. Be sure to account for inflation." He recommends a book he gave to his children, *The Armchair Millionaire*, by Lewis Schiff, Douglas Gerlach, and Kate Hanley (Atria, 2002).

## Roger: Where Did He Go Wrong?

Roger Bell, by contrast, constantly struggles with his money, his investments, and his emotions. He's been an on-again, off-again client of our firm. Frankly, we have taken him back several times against our better judgment, hoping he will get his life straightened out. But his pattern continues. He opens an account, gets frustrated, loses his patience, and then fires us. Sometime later, almost like clockwork, he calls us back saying he needs our help because he can't stand what happens when he manages his own money. He tells us he has learned his lesson this time and that now things will be different.

Like George, Roger retired with what would seem to be plenty of money to live a good life. But he suffered a series of significant investment losses as he followed his own investment whims. The losses resulted not from choosing bad strategies, but from repeatedly shifting from one investment plan to another, never giving any strategy enough time to work properly. Against our advice, Roger is essentially addicted to chasing recent hot performance, trying in vain to find some spectacularly successful investment that will let him recover his past losses. And as his losses accumulate, recovery becomes harder and harder to achieve.

When he has been our client, Roger has invested in sensible strategies that are likely to meet his needs over the long run. But he can't seem to accept short-term setbacks and has never been patient enough to let long-term strategies work. Ironically, Roger's fear of not making enough money has led him to make investments in which he has lost a lot of money. Intellectually, Roger understands all this. But he can't get the emotional part of it right.

When we manage Roger's money, he is constantly watching for anything that he perceives as a mistake. When he manages his own money, he is either wildly overconfident (when his latest investment has gone up in value) or quite depressed (when his latest investment has gone down). Roger does not have any long-term plan that I'm aware of. He hasn't figured out his risk tolerance. And as far as I know, over the past 12 years he has lost more money than he has gained. On the outside, his life looks prosperous. He drives a nice car, lives in a nice home, and has a fabulous boat. But on the inside, his anxiety over his finances poisons his ability to be satisfied.

Roger's wife, Joyce, has a separate account that we manage for her without any input from her husband. She has much more patience and a long-term attitude. It's no surprise that she's more successful and happier. When we talk to Roger, we don't hear many happy stories about his life. Roger's approach to his money has led to some serious fights between him and Joyce, who has found it nearly impossible to be a supportive partner to him.

Even after the losses he has taken, Roger still could live quite comfortably, even if he put all his money into certificates of deposit, which I have suggested to him more than once. But he doesn't. In the end, Roger's money has become a problem for him instead of a tool to give him a life he wants to live.

I hope this book will help you be more like George and less like Roger!

# 3

# Lessons from Smart People

*What the wise do in the beginning, fools do in the end.*

—Warren Buffett

Successful retirement requires something more than just raw financial numbers. That's obvious from the stories of George and Roger, the two retirees we met in Chapter 2. Each one ended his working life with more than enough money, yet they wound up in very different places. Left to their own devices, most people will find themselves somewhere between the two opposites of George, who seems to have done just about everything right, and Roger, who has not managed to have a successful retirement in spite of starting out with plenty of money.

In four decades of helping and watching people manage their money, before and during retirement, I've had a chance to observe how the smartest people I know deal with retirement. It boils down to this: Smart people take a thoughtful, long-term approach to their lives. They avoid extremes, more often than not choosing middle-of-the road investment strategies. They regard their money as a tool, not as the center of their lives. They have plenty of things to live for and they look for ways to connect positively with other people.

## Smart Step 1

Smart people make plans for their retirement, financial and otherwise, and they put those plans in writing. It has always puzzled me why people will spend days planning a two-week vacation (and in some cases will spend months planning a half-day wedding and reception), yet those same people will make five-figure and even six-figure investment decisions on a whim. An article published in *Fortune* magazine in 1999 reported on a study which found that investors who had made written plans by age 40 wound up on average with five times as much money by age 65 as those who didn't have written plans.

Of course, the act of writing a plan doesn't put money in anybody's pocket. And even the most brilliant plan is worthless if it collects dust on a shelf. But people who are methodical enough to put their plans into writing are also likely to do many of the other things that lead to successful investing.

That's one of the key points of this book: A successful retirement doesn't result from one or two acts of genius; it results from attitudes and habits cultivated over the years. With a written plan, you can get back on course when you go astray. Without a plan, you don't even have a reliable way to determine whether you are off course.

## Smart Step 2

Smart people, before and during retirement, don't spend much of their time on the proverbial porch rocking in the proverbial chair. Instead they keep themselves active and challenged, both mentally and physically. It's no secret that people who use their brains live longer than those who are intellectually lazy. There are lots of enjoyable ways to do this, including reading, crossword puzzles, and taking (or teaching) a class. Travel is another excellent way to keep the mind and body in good shape. The smartest and happiest people I know are invariably interested in and curious about many things. They never stop wanting to learn new ways to understand the world and interact with it.

Physical activity is also a great way to enhance your retirement. Whether it's climbing mountains or just walking around the block, smart people remain physically active to whatever extent they can.

## Smart Step 3

Smart people cultivate new relationships and nurture their established ones with friends, family, and colleagues. I've worked with many retired people and I've noticed that the happiest ones seem to have many favorite people in their lives, including people younger than they are. These happy retirees are invariably interested in other people and seem to take a delight in finding ways to do favors, not for credit or appreciation but for the satisfaction of being able to help make life better for somebody else.

In the end, life can sweep away our dignity and our money. But if we have friends and family members with whom we can share joy, pain, and respect, we are blessed. This is something that money cannot buy.

## Smart Step 4

Smart people have lots to live for. They wouldn't have any trouble making a list of two dozen things they would like to do if they had time—places to go, people to see, books to read, new things to learn.

## Smart Step 5

Smart investors and retirees pay attention to their money and treat it as if it were precious. This seems so obvious that you may wonder why I'd bother to mention it in a book like this. Here's why: I've seen too many people, including many with high incomes, treat money as if it were an unlimited resource, almost like water flowing into their lives at the twist of a tap. These people seem to barely notice when money leaves their pockets.

Thomas Stanley, chairman of the Affluent Market Institute in Atlanta, spent 30 years studying wealthy people and how they got that way. He observed that the typical wealthy person is likely to have lived in the same city for many years and to live in a middle-class neighborhood next door to people much less wealthy. Stanley says great wealth builders spend plenty of time planning their investments. They would rather spend money on good financial advice than on a new boat. The least effective wealth builders are those who turn their important financial decisions over to other people.

The key word in that last sentence is *decisions.* I believe most investors can benefit from professional advice and management. But nobody can give you the best advice or management unless you have made some critical decisions about the risks you are willing to take and how you will manage those risks. If you delegate such important choices to somebody else, you are inviting mistakes that can lead to major disappointments and bitterness—and the possible derailment of your long-term objectives.

I recommend that you spend as much time as it takes to understand your investment needs and establish a plan that will make your money work hard for you. And then I hope you will set that plan on automatic pilot so you can concentrate on enjoying life.

## Smart Step 6

Smart people don't wait for luck to make them wealthy (see box). Instead, they cultivate habits and attitudes that improve the odds of their success. They spend less than they can afford to on vacations, houses, cars, and entertainment. They put their money to work building wealth, not building lifestyles that saddle them with expenses and debt.

---

### Luck

One of the best quotes on luck I ever heard was from talk show host Dave Ramsey: "Good things happen to people who are doing all the right things. That is how luck gets created."

My own take on luck is this: Things happen that people regard simply as good luck. But something transforms a random event into an opportunity. That "something" is the spark that's critical. If you can recognize a circumstance as an opportunity, and if you're prepared to take advantage of it, then it's a lucky break. But if the same thing happened to somebody else who didn't recognize it as an opportunity, or who didn't have the resources or the ability to capitalize on it, then it's just a random event without meaning.

If you "do all the right things," as Dave Ramsey says, you'll improve your chances of getting a lucky break. And ironically, if you're doing all the right things, you won't have so much need for that lucky break.

## Smart Step 7

Smart people who are planning retirement don't shortchange themselves and their futures. They don't buy the notion that they will be able to get by on only 70 percent of their preretirement income. They have lots of things they want to do, and they want the means to fully participate in everything they can. About half of our clients spend more during retirement than they did while they were working. When that doesn't jeopardize their future plans, we encourage them to do it.

## Smart Step 8

Smart people don't burden themselves with a heap of consumer debt. Sure, most folks need credit to buy a house, which can turn out to be a fine investment. And most working people need loans to buy vehicles. But revolving credit is like a nasty drug habit that keeps people enslaved and prevents them from being independent.

Credit cards aren't inherently bad. If you can pay off your balance every month, you can get some nice freebies, whether it's frequent flyer miles, a cash rebate, or a donation to a favorite charity. But if you just make the minimum payments, you'll probably be sorry. And you'll almost certainly forget what you spent the money on before it's paid for. With a credit card and a free-spending attitude, it's easy to rack up a balance of $3,000 in an afternoon. Even if you never charge another dime, at a typical monthly payment rate of 2 percent of the balance coupled with an annual interest rate of 16.5 percent, it could take you 30 years—and payments of nearly $8,500—to finally pay for that $3,000 spending spree.

## Smart Step 9

Smart people know the value of time, and they don't wait until the last minute to start planning and saving for retirement. If you're in your twenties, retirement seems pretty remote. Yet that's exactly the point: All that time is what gives you the opportunity to do a lot with a little.

If you can manage to contribute $5,000 every year into a Roth IRA starting when you're 25, and if you get a 10 percent return, by age 60 you'll have roughly $1.5 million. But if you wait until you're 40 to start making those contributions, you'll have only about

$320,000 when you're 60. If you look at it another way, a one-time investment of $5,000 when you're 25 will grow (at 10 percent) to $140,512 by the time you're 60. Wait until you're 40 and you'll have to start with $20,886 to get the same result. Wait until you're 50, and you'll have to start with $54,173.

## Smart Step 10

Smart people who have waited too long don't try to play catch-up by investing in high-risk ventures that rely on luck to make up for lost time. Instead, they find ways to save more and scale back their retirement needs. If necessary, they plan to work longer while they build their assets in a sensible way. If they take extra investment risk, they do so thoughtfully and carefully.

### Thinking About Risk

Risk is a central topic that deserves investors' attention, and it's worthy of another thoughtful discussion here. The markets reward investors who assume prudent risks, and the way you handle this will have a big impact on how successful you are as a long-term investor.

Most of us have no direct control over the external events that affect our investments. But we can control how we respond to them. To a greater or lesser extent, all of us struggle internally in a battle between intellect and emotion—between our fear and greed on the one hand and our discipline and reason on the other. Very few among us are so disciplined that our reason always rules our actions. This plays out in the stock market every day. Because we must invest for a future that we cannot know, there is simply no way we can escape taking risks.

Here's something I wrote to my company's clients in 1998 and again in 2000, in both cases when the market had unexpectedly turned downward: "In the good times, it seems as if investing is about accepting wealth. You put down your money, almost like planting it in a garden, and watch it grow. But in fact, in good times and bad, investing is really about managing risk and managing your emotions. To be a successful investor, you have to do at least a decent job at both those tasks."

Managing risk is the hardest part of investing. The best way to start is to understand what risk really is. Mathematical definitions of risk are good for measuring and comparing risks. But they don't get at the heart of how real people actually experience risk. The *American Heritage Dictionary* defines risk as "the possibility of suffering harm or loss." Other definitions use the words *danger, uncertainty,* and *hazard.*

Here's my own definition: Risk is a possibility that you invite into your life in which you could lose something important. That something could be your physical safety, a relationship, or money.

My definition of risk, while unconventional, is carefully crafted to make a couple of important points. The word *invite* makes it quite clear that risk is not imposed on you from the outside. On the contrary, it results from a choice you make.

Let me use an analogy. When you invite a guest into your home, you are taking some level of risk. There's always the possibility that your guest could take something or damage something or be rude to you or your family or to other guests who may be present. Experience may make you pretty sure this won't happen, but it is a possibility, and you are the one who invited that guest.

Just as you choose to invite someone into your home, prudent investment risk is something you accept and knowingly choose.

Second, this definition makes it clear that risk is not theoretical. We measure it in this book in terms of statistics, but risk is about actually *losing* something important. (I wish more teenage drivers understood this concept!)

Why would anybody willingly take the risk of losing something important? Because that's what investors get paid to do. In general, the more risk you are willing to take, the more return you may possibly receive. However, this is true only when you take intelligent risks based on understanding. It doesn't apply to random risks based on bravado or recent hot performance.

There are two categories of risk: *objective* risk, which can be measured, and *emotional* risk, which depends on each person's perceptions.

Imagine you are shopping for a certificate of deposit (CD). The easiest place to get a CD is your own bank. But it's highly unlikely that your bank just happens to have the very best deal in the country. If you want to do business with the folks down the block who know you, you'll have to accept whatever interest rate your bank pays. Alternatively, you can shop around and perhaps find a higher interest rate at a bank 1,000 miles away.

Objectively, the risk is identical. Each CD has the same U.S. government backing. But the distant bank may hold more emotional risk. You can't walk into a branch and talk to the manager. You may never know anybody there except by phone. But because the distant bank pays higher interest, you are in effect earning a premium return for the small amount of emotional risk you take by banking there.

It's easy to measure the risk of past investments, as we discuss in some detail in Chapter 10. After the fact, it's pretty easy to say, "I could handle that," because you know how it turned out. But when you contemplate the next

*(Continued)*

30 years, you're looking risk straight in the eyes, because you have no idea what's ahead. That's why I often say, "There's no risk in the past. The only risk is in the future."

Getting risk right is a balancing act. Take too much, and you can compromise your future by incurring big losses that you can't afford. Take too little, and you can compromise your future by depriving yourself of the return you need.

To determine if you are taking enough risk, ask yourself this: Are my investments providing the return that I need to meet my goals, with a margin left over for error? If the answer is yes, you are probably taking enough risk and don't need to take more.

To determine whether you have assumed too much risk, ask yourself three questions:

1. Have I lost any sleep over my investments?
2. Do I feel compelled to watch the financial news and check fund prices daily or weekly? (We are talking about feeling compelled, not just curious.)
3. Does the financial news make me worry about my future?

If your answer to any of those questions is yes, you may have taken on too much risk. If you answer yes to all three, your investments are definitely too risky for you.

## Smart Step 11

Smart people learn from the mistakes of other people so they don't have to repeat them. Virtually everything I've put into this book is based on mistakes I've seen people make. If you learn the lessons here, their pain can become your gain.

## Smart Step 12

I think I've saved the best lesson for last. This may seem to contradict everything you've read so far, but it fits. Smart people don't wait for retirement to start making their dreams come true. Smart people accept the fact that life is uncertain and all the tomorrows we assume will be there can be snatched away in an instant. With wealth set aside for their futures and with their goals and dreams clearly identified, the really smart folks I know are always looking for ways to turn those dreams into reality, starting now.

Here's an exercise: Imagine you have somehow acquired a huge amount of money, and you'll never have to work again. The interesting question in this exercise is not how you'd spend your money but how you'd spend your time—because that, in essence, is your life.

Now write down four or five major things you would like to devote time and energy to for the rest of your life. Maybe it's going back to school, learning how to fly a plane, or honing your skills at a hobby or avocation. Maybe you'd love to be a philanthropist or live in a foreign culture and learn a new language. The object is to identify what you would do if you could do anything. Then find ways to pursue those interests now. Do it for immediate satisfaction and as preparation for when you'll have more time. For almost anything on your list, you can find ways to indulge your passion without waiting for retirement. If you do that, you'll improve your quality of life now—and after you have retired.

# 4

# The Psychology of Successful Investing

*We are what we repeatedly do. Excellence, then, comes not from our actions but from our habits.*

—Aristotle

It's relatively easy to prescribe an investment plan that is likely to work well if it's followed diligently. Much of this book is devoted to doing just that. The hard part is keeping yourself from derailing your own plans. One of the biggest mistakes investors make is underestimating the power of their emotions. If you take the time to understand the psychology of successful investing, you'll make your life more pleasant and you'll probably have more money to spend in retirement and leave to your heirs. But if you ignore this topic, I promise you will pay for doing so.

Many investors get in and out of the stock market from time to time depending on whether they think prices are relatively high or relatively low. Some have mechanical timing systems to guide them, but many people believe they can successfully make their own decisions about when to get in and when to get out. In hindsight, the majority of such moves are counterproductive.

When stock prices are relatively high, financial risk is also high and the opportunity for gains relatively low. Yet high prices, ironically, mean low emotional risk for investors. People find it easy to buy investments that have been going up. Conversely, when stock prices are relatively low, financial risk is also low; the opportunity for gains is high. But low prices mean high emotional risk. Again ironically, investors find it hard to buy low-priced investments that have been beaten up in the market.

There's no getting around one very basic truth about investing: The way to make money is to buy low and sell high. But our emotions, by trying to bring us comfort, work against us and try to persuade us to do the opposite. In the short run, comfort is very gratifying. But in the long run, comfort always has a cost.

Investors who crave quick, easy answers and uninterrupted peace of mind should expect lower long-term returns. Think about diet and exercise. It's no great mystery how to eat sensibly and exercise regularly. There's little dispute that doing so makes people healthier, happier, and likely to live longer. But knowing the right things to do is not enough. To get results you must somehow get yourself to actually do the right things, while you avoid doing counterproductive things.

Psychology is the key. If you just do what you feel like, you'll most likely eat too much, you'll eat the wrong things, and you won't exercise as you should. What "feels good" at the moment is usually a lousy guide to what's really in your best interest. This is just as true of investing as it is of eating.

Throughout your life as an investor, you will be goaded by the media, which will do its best to keep stimulating you with entertainment that's carefully disguised to look like insight and advice. The aim of the media is not to help you. It's to keep you coming back for more—to deliver your attention to advertisers. Unless you realize this, you will be constantly misled.

You can be sure that the investment profession understands psychology very well. If you let them, investment professionals will be only too happy to take advantage of you. Wall Street doesn't really care how you invest your money. The industry's primary goal is to get you to change whatever you're doing. That's how Wall Street makes money. To that end, investors are barraged night and day with sales pitches, some obvious and some masquerading as objective investment advice or insight. All of it is designed to get people to buy and sell. If you aspire to be a successful investor, you'll have to figure out how to deal with all that.

Investing is in some ways like driving a car. The route you need to take may be pretty straightforward, but your attitude, skills, and psychological makeup will play a major role in shaping your actual experience of the journey. When it's your money at stake, you should be the one in the driver's seat, even if you are taking directions from someone else. The best way to keep your hands on the wheel is to have a plan that will work for you, and then stick to that plan. And the best way to do that is to recognize the difference between your financial needs and your emotional needs.

If you are an investor, from time to time you will experience setbacks, confusion, frustration, uncertainty, anxiety, and disappointment. How you respond to events and to your emotions will have a big impact on your success, or lack of it. Your investment plan will be more likely to succeed if it is designed to use your psychological strengths and overcome your weak spots. This chapter will show you some useful tools to keep your emotions from leading you down the wrong path. However, only you can apply those tools and keep yourself on the right path.

Ultimately, the solution to many investors' psychological challenges is pretty simple. Because your emotions will never be a reliable guide, your best bet is to put it all on automatic. That means automatic savings, automatic investing, automatic asset allocation, automatic rebalancing, and automatic distributions in retirement.

## Cruising the Investment Highway

There's an interesting parallel between the way people drive and the way they invest their money. Good drivers practice defensive driving techniques. If you know what to look out for on the highway, you can greatly improve your chances of getting to your destination safely.

I want you to be a good defensive investor. To do that, there are three things you need to watch out for: your own emotions, the manipulations of Wall Street, and the misleading media. On one level, investing is about knowing the right things to do, and then doing them. In this book, I teach you the right things to do—but I can't make you do them.

In the real world, investors are often driven more by emotions than by logic. Mark Hulbert, a *New York Times* and Dow Jones's *MarketWatch* columnist whose business has been to study investment newsletters since 1980, said it well during an interview on my company's radio show: "Our intellect is basically no match for our emotions. As we see over and over, emotions will trump the intellect almost every single time."

As an investor, your emotional adversaries are likely to be fear, greed, impatience, and frustration. How you deal with them will have a huge effect on how much money you are at risk of losing.

Impatience can be deadly. In traffic jams, impatient drivers often pay lots of attention to what lane they are in and how other lanes are doing in relation to theirs. If another lane seems to be moving faster, they will swerve over to cut in front of somebody else. Some drivers do this repeatedly, taking every opportunity to gain some small advantage for themselves. Those drivers may gain a few seconds here and there. But in the process, they raise the level of danger and annoyance to themselves and everybody around them. In investment terms, drivers like that take on much more risk in return for uncertain (and often elusive) gains.

Impatient investors often watch the market like hawks. They want results, and they want them now. Impatient investors are easy prey for the investment industry. They can be lured to change lanes, then change lanes again, always seeking a competitive advantage. Unfortunately they often wind up as roadkill, retiring to the shoulder of the road with their capital in money market funds while their more patient counterparts build wealth in the slower lane.

Patient investors may wait for decades before they reap their rewards. But they are more likely to be able to retire comfortably—and more likely to sleep better along the way.

## Your Style in the Driver's Seat

When you drive, you have a certain style. You may not notice your style, but I promise you that the people who ride with you do. There's a certain amount of frustration you are willing to tolerate from other drivers who don't behave as you think they should. And there's a way you react when that frustration exceeds your limit.

On a clogged freeway, do you weave from lane to lane or rush to the next exit, hoping to find a better route that other drivers haven't discovered? Many people change their investments mainly to relieve frustration. The odds of success are not in their favor.

## Watch Out for Your Expectations

An important part of dealing with your emotions is managing your expectations. Of course you want to make money from your investments. And if you follow a sound investment plan, you will. But I can guarantee this: You won't make money all the time. Unless your investments are limited to Treasury bills or other cash equivalents, your investments will at some point go down in value. What matters is not *whether* that happens but how you deal with it when it does.

In fact, you should hope you don't make big gains on your investments right away. The reason is psychological, not financial. If you make a lot of money quickly after you invest in something, it is almost always a random event. But to your mind, that random event will seem very important if it happens in the first hours, days, or weeks of your investment.

I've observed over the years that investors are much more likely to stick with investments that reward them very early in the game. If a fund shoots up 10 or 20 percent in the first six months you own it, at some level you will develop an emotional bond with it. This bond will cloud your judgment. No longer will this fund be merely a tool that you use to accomplish something. Instead, it will have become an ally or a friend, something you feel you can trust to take care of you.

It's ironic, but even the best investment plan in the world can have very little emotional appeal if it loses money in the first six months that you own it. You can easily develop an emotional aversion to it and start to regard this investment not as a tool but as a bad idea, a sort of adversary that gives you bad vibes.

Here's another trick your mind may play on you: Wall Street spends hundreds of millions of dollars every year to try to make you put your trust in names that seem safe, familiar, and dependable. If a specific mutual fund is mentioned in the media in a favorable light enough times, millions of people are likely to have a positive impression of it, even though most of them could not explain why. And this impression has staying power.

From 1970 through 1992, Janus Fund achieved a 16 percent compound rate of return. That and the resulting publicity helped it become one of the nation's largest growth funds in the mid 1990s. Long after this fund's performance fell, its favorable impression persisted and money kept pouring in. Not until the bear market of 2000 through 2002 did the popular perception of the Janus Fund finally fall into line with the reality that this flagship offering was, at best, an average long-term performer.

## Your Goals Should Be Good

One of your most important psychological allies will be a set of smart, sensible goals. Many people say their objective is to beat the market. But I don't really believe that, and I'll tell you why. If all you want is to beat the market, then in a year when the market (however you define it) is down 40 percent, you should be supremely happy to lose only 35 percent of your money. Do you know anybody who would brag to his family about losing 35 percent? I don't. In a good year, if the market is up 30 percent, you'd be compelled to complain to your family if your portfolio went up only 28 percent, as if you were a failure.

If you aren't clear about your objectives, you can experience anxiety no matter what results you get. To investors, anxiety is a powerful force that can tempt you to switch investments when you shouldn't.

Veteran investors know that the market does not reward all investors at the same time. Older investors should want higher stock prices so they can convert their investments into cash for living expenses. Younger investors should want lower prices so they can buy a piece of the future at a reduced price.

What should your objective be? There's no right answer for everyone. The only wrong answer is to have no answer, or to believe that you can and should achieve every possible financial goal at the same time.

## Watch Out for Wall Street

Even when you have your own emotions under control, you've still got to deal with Wall Street. Managing risks is at the heart of successful investing, and you should always focus your attention on this when you're considering a new investment. But you'll rarely find a broker who wants you to do that. The investment industry has learned that when people confront the emotions associated with losing money, most folks will flee before a salesperson can make a dime in commissions.

The industry doesn't want to talk about preparing you for the inevitable bad times, even though that is what you need. The industry just wants to make money while there's money to be made. That happens when commissions are generated, and commissions are generated when you do something.

Optimism sells, and it's no accident that Wall Street is organized to make you think that higher returns in your portfolio can be just a transaction away. If you just sit tight, nobody makes much money. Everybody in the business has a better idea for what you should do with your money, and they're all eager to do it for you.

As investors, we can choose from among thousands of mutual funds, thousands of managers, and thousands of individual stocks, as well as many other financial products and plans. It's easy to be a frequent trader. If you wake up in the middle of the night with an investment idea or fear, you can find a broker who will execute a trade for you immediately on the Tokyo or London exchanges.

The industry is highly motivated and highly trained (to say nothing of highly compensated) to do whatever it takes to get your money under management. Competition is fierce, and the sales and marketing forces will use every trick they can to lure you to sign on the dotted line.

There is an exception, one that's not necessarily to your advantage. Very few brokers and investment managers are completely immune to the pain of investing. Not many of them like to have to deal with clients who have sustained major losses. But even this compassion, if you want to call it that, works against investors. Brokers and portfolio managers sometimes shy away from delivering the bad news to clients. In the 1987 stock market crash, thousands of brokers found their phones were ringing off the hooks. Many of them coped with the situation by simply leaving their offices.

We saw the effects of denial and inaction during the bear market of 2000 through 2002. Hundreds of thousands of investors failed to protect themselves while their technology-heavy stock portfolios eroded. In many cases, people's retirement dreams were shattered.

## Managing Investment Pain

When people are in severe pain, whether it's physical, emotional, or financial, they often lose the ability to make good decisions. Stopping the hurt can become the top priority, sometimes regardless of consequences that will show up later.

Investing money should be about ultimate consequences, not about feeling good today. Many investors act as if the opposite were true. Decisions based on pain and emotions are almost always counterproductive. That's one reason it's extremely valuable to have a plan you can turn to when things start to hurt.

Various strategies for managing investment pain may work well for one person and not for another. Here's my own plan for managing pain. I have two types of investments. The first is money that I don't expect I will ever need for myself or my family. This money is under my control, but I intend that someday it will go to my children. I'm not counting on departing this world any time soon, and I've allocated this money aggressively, in some cases using leverage. I'm shooting for an average annual total return of 15 to 20 percent. I think this is a reasonable goal for aggressive investors with a high tolerance for risk, and that's appropriate for this money.

My pain threshold for this money is a loss of 30 percent in one year. I want to make sure you understand that any loss at all will be painful to me, and a loss of 30 percent would be very uncomfortable. I am willing to continue these investments knowing that I could lose that much, though I think it's highly unlikely that will happen.

My other investments are for my immediate family and my own retirement. I know that I can reach my personal financial goals if I continue to earn at least 8 percent, compounded. My goal is to achieve a 10 percent return, giving me a substantial margin for error.

My pain tolerance for this money is more limited. I have what you could call a "bag lady" personality, worrying (not very rationally) that I might run out of money before I run out of life. With this retirement money, I am willing to accept no more than a 10 percent annual loss.

What happens if my losses exceed my thresholds? In either case, losses greater than my threshold would cause me to reevaluate my whole strategy. A loss outside my limits would indicate that circumstances had changed beyond what I understand now. And it would mean my carefully crafted strategies had become inadequate to deal with that new reality.

This would put me into unknown territory, and I am not certain how I would respond. I suspect one of my first responses would be to start saving more money each month to try to make up for the loss. And I certainly would consider taking a less aggressive investment posture in the future, perhaps putting more emphasis on bonds and less on equities.

I suggest you determine your own pain threshold. Reduce it to numbers if you can. This will require you to understand yourself, and that can be beneficial in itself. Remember, when you pass your pain threshold, your perception will be less reliable and your decisions more risky. That's when you want to be able to take a written plan out of your desk drawer or file cabinet.

## Watch Out for the Media

Anxiety is one of your main enemies as an investor, and it can be inflamed by the financial media. The job of the media is not to look out for your interests and make you a better investor. Perhaps you think the folks at *Money* magazine have done your homework for you. Unfortunately, that's not how it really works. In real life, the job of the media is to keep your attention for the benefit of advertisers. But it's even worse than that: Many of the articles in financial publications were spawned in the public relations departments of mutual fund companies, brokerage houses, and other firms that make and sell financial products.

Media companies learned long ago that it's next to impossible to sell magazines, newspapers, and television shows unless they have something new, different, exciting, and better. Which would you pick up first—a magazine promising to tell you about a hot new investment, or a magazine with a cover story saying a 25-year-old investment plan is still the best one?

Every hour, every day, every week, every month the media have to hawk something new and different. If you are persuaded to buy a fund or a stock this month, you've got to be tempted to do something else next month. Otherwise, you'll be just one less reader (or listener or viewer) who can be delivered to advertisers next month.

The media offer a parade of experts who slice and dice every part of the financial world before your eyes and ears, often 24 hours a day. And how useful are all these experts? Not very. For any financial topic you can think of, I could find at least two highly qualified experts who would take opposite positions on the meaning of any particular situation. The media like to quote these people's views as if they were facts instead of interpretations and guesses.

Some big brokerage houses employ people whose only job is to answer media questions about the pulse of the market. None of these people has any reliable way to know why the market is doing whatever it's doing. But does that stop them? Not a bit!

Consider the following imaginary dialogue, which could pass for wisdom and insight at any financial broadcasting concern:

Anchor: "John, why are investors reacting this way?"
Guest: "Well, Carol, I think people are nervous about what the
        Fed might do at its next meeting."
Anchor: "Thanks, John."

Thanks? Thanks for what? John's comment says absolutely nothing. Yet if it were on tape it could be dropped into any broadcast at any time on any day picked at random. And it would be absolutely right at home in the blather that makes up financial broadcast journalism.

## You Can't Separate Strategy from the Broader Market

I want to tell you a story about a client who couldn't separate his carefully plotted strategy from what was happening in the broader market.

After extensive discussions with this very smart client, we set up a worldwide balanced account for him with four equally weighted categories of assets: U.S. stocks, U.S. bonds, international stocks, and international bonds. We expected this mix would give him just the right combination of limited risk along with reasonable expected returns that would meet his needs. There was no question that he completely understood what we were doing.

About six months later, he called to say he was quite upset that his account was underperforming the Dow Jones Industrial Average, which had been doing quite well and which had been in the media spotlight. On a rational level, this client's complaint made no sense. Half his portfolio was in bonds, and only 12.5 percent was invested in large-cap U.S. stocks like the

30 that make up the Dow Jones index. There was no way his portfolio could mirror the Dow. What could he have been expecting?

When I reminded him that we purposely set up his account to make sure it did not match the Dow, he assured me he understood that on an intellectual level. But his anxiety was not based on reason. His emotional side told him that he had come to an investment professional for money management, and now he felt as if we were not on top of his account and the market.

His emotional reaction was akin to turning on your car radio when you are stuck in traffic on a freeway, and then getting angry when you hear that several other freeways are wide open. It's an understandable reaction, but not very rational and not very useful. We worked through this issue with him, and in the end he stuck with his carefully crafted plan.

## The Two Lists

Many people think they have to figure out whether the market is too high or too low. But can they do it? Let me describe a mental exercise I do for fun every now and then, one I often present in my workshops. I call it "the two lists."

The folks on Wall Street always have an "A" list of reasons the market is almost certainly going up and a "B" list of reasons it's almost certainly headed downward. Every item on each list is plausible and seems important. I usually believe everything on each one. The problem is that much of the time, the A list is just as solid as the B list, and vice versa. All the changing and conflicting items on these lists give you no rational basis for making investment decisions.

For example, here's an abbreviated version of the two lists that I compiled early in 2008:

**A.** *Reasons the market will go up:* The U.S. dollar is relatively low, making our products available at bargain prices internationally. The low dollar also is great for the U.S. tourism industry, attracting lots of Europeans, Asians, and others. Stocks of U.S. companies are also relative bargains for foreign investors, a factor that could increase demand. The Federal Reserve has a huge incentive to prop up U.S. banks. Interest rates are relatively low and heading downward, making it easier for individuals and corporations to finance needed projects. Employment is high by historical standards. Worldwide economic growth is expected to be 4.5 percent this year. This is a presidential election year, historically a bullish indicator for the stock market.

**B.** *Reasons the market will go down:* Energy prices are soaring, hurting consumers and all sorts of businesses. Expectations for corporate profits are falling. Fear of a recession is widespread. The subprime banking mess may turn out to have very long-lasting repercussions, much like the savings-and-loan meltdown of the late 1980s and early 1990s. Home foreclosures are higher than they have been in years, limiting the ability of many people to invest in the market and fuel our consumer-driven economy. Inflation is heating up at the same time that the economy is cooling down. The low value of the U.S. dollar effectively increases the cost of everything we import. It also may discourage foreign investors from continuing to finance the U.S. treasury.

Each of those lists could be expanded by a mile. If you had to choose one of them, how would you do it?

Unfortunately, many investors don't know what they believe or why they believe it. As a result, they adopt a view of the market based on who they heard when they happened to be in a receptive mood. For no reason I've ever understood, many people give particular credence to what they hear from somebody sitting next to them in an airplane. I hate to think how many people make major financial decisions based on somebody's personality or charm.

## The Answer

The right way to deal with most broadcast financial journalism is to either change the station or turn off the radio or TV. The wrong way, as I stated in Chapter 1, is to make investment moves based on what you see or hear on these programs.

Here's the straight scoop: From time to time you will know exactly what you ought to do as an investor—and you simply won't want to do it. The most basic investment decision is the one you face when you have some money that you could either set aside or spend. Particularly if you have a family, there will be times when you'll want to spend that money instead of save it.

To invest money requires postponing gratification. This is an ability (or willingness) that signifies a level of maturity. If you can't learn to do that, you will never be much of an investor. If your savings plan depends on how you feel every time you get a paycheck, that plan doesn't have much of a chance.

Solution: Put your investments on automatic pilot. Have money deducted from your paycheck and deposited into a 401(k) account or automatically withdrawn from your bank account and put into a mutual fund's automatic investment plan. Make this decision once, not every time you get paid. Pay yourself first (before you spend any money), and pay yourself automatically.

There will be times when you'll want to follow some interesting tip or idea you hear about. Don't do it. To remove (or at least greatly reduce) temptation, make sure your new investments are automatically being allocated in the right way. There will be times when you won't want to go to the trouble of rebalancing. If you can, make this happen automatically once a year. Your best defense against your emotions and against the influences of Wall Street and the media is to get things figured out once, then let other people and their computers carry out your wishes. That will make your life a lot more pleasant. And it will certainly make you a better investor.

# CHAPTER 5

# Who Are You and What Are Your Goals?

*If you don't know who you are, the stock market is an expensive place to find out.*

—George Goodman

This book contains the information, insights, and directions necessary for investors to thrive. But these tools won't help you unless you apply them properly to your own circumstances. This chapter tells you how to do that by estimating some important mileposts on your journey to financial independence. To make your money do more for you, it's first necessary to answer the question "more of what?" This question is trickier than you might think, because it depends on the interplay of several important things that only you can figure out.

To get a good handle on your own circumstances, the most important figure is the income you will need the first year you retire. The word *need* is critical. Your basic needs—food, clothing, shelter, and medical care—must be met no matter what. We call this figure your base target. You'll also want to compute a second target annual retirement income that would be enough to support your desires for such nonessential things as travel, a second home, and leaving a substantial estate. We call this figure your live-it-up target, because it represents the grander life you want to live.

Once you have determined those two numbers, you can figure out how much retirement income must come from your investments to reach each of these targets. Then you can easily calculate a ballpark figure for how big your portfolio should be when you retire. If you're still working with 10 or more years to go before retirement, this ballpark figure is probably good enough to direct your investing for the time being. When you get close to retirement, you'll want to fine tune the numbers and think seriously about how you'll withdraw the money. We take up that topic in Chapter 13.

Early in my retirement workshops, I ask for a show of hands in the audience to get people to start thinking about their primary investment goals. "How many of you want to beat the market?" Some hands always go up. "How many of you want to get the highest return you can get within your risk tolerance?" Lots of hands. "Who wants to find the lowest-risk way to meet your needs?" A few hands go up.

By this time, I can see a little uncertainty on people's faces. Each one of these goals seems pretty attractive, and often investors think they want to achieve them all. They want to beat the market; they want high returns; and they want low risks. Some people are primarily competitive. They'll most likely choose beating the market. Others are oriented toward return, while still others are oriented toward security and safety.

This much I know: You can't successfully pursue all three of these goals at once, at least not with the same pool of money. You've got to choose, and you should do it purposefully. If you don't have a focus, Wall Street will be happy to create one for you. It will invariably be whatever the investment industry has decided is the current path of least resistance to selling you something.

Almost all the advertisements for financial services stress beating the market. They may call it doing better or getting performance. But I don't think you'll find many ads that promote being like the crowd. However, as we saw in Chapter 4, beating the market isn't all it's cracked up to be.

Most of the participants in my workshops arrive with their hearts set on getting the highest returns they can. And what could be wrong with that? Nothing, actually, except that you might not make it. If all you want is the highest possible return, watch the big billboards for the national mega-lottery. When the jackpot gets up over $200 million, invest your money in tickets. The payoff will be so high that no financial calculator will be able to compute your percentage return. You say that's not exactly what you had in mind? Oh! That's why I tell people to never, ever say you're looking for the highest possible return without adding "within my risk tolerance."

The third possible objective, finding the lowest-risk way to meet your needs, is very attractive. I wish it were easier to accomplish. It's easier (and more pleasant) to figure out the return that you want than it is to determine how much risk you can take. The first is a function of mathematics, the second a function of emotions. But it's equally valuable to know your risk tolerance, because it's easier to do something about it.

For example, if you tell me you can tolerate no more than a 15 percent one-year loss, it's relatively easy for me to prescribe a mix of investments with enough risk that you're likely to lose 15 percent in some future 12-month period. Or, if you tell me you need an annualized return of 10 percent over 20 or 30 years, I can suggest investments that have achieved that long-term return in the past. But your objective should be to obtain a long-term cumulative result, and it could take decades before you will know for sure whether you succeeded.

On your way to the long-term future, you must get through the short-term future. In the first 12 months after you begin an investment plan, your return could be a gain of 30 percent or a loss of 15 percent. You won't complain about the gain, but how can I show you that your 15 percent loss is part of a long-term annualized 10 percent return? I can't!

The upshot is that I recommend you do your best to estimate both your need for return and your tolerance for risk. We focus on risk tolerance in Chapter 10, where you'll learn exactly how to find an investment mix that will come close to meeting your needs for safety and for return. In this chapter, we look at how to determine how much money you need in order to retire. That way you will know what you must do between now and then.

In my workshop, I ask people what annual return they want. I give them a range of choices, from under 8 percent all the way up to 15 percent and above. It won't surprise you to hear that people typically prefer higher returns to lower ones. I then ask what return they need. Most of them don't know. Because this second number is critical, I want to walk you through the drill to figure it out. This exercise will give you only a ballpark figure at best. But unless you are on the brink of retirement or already retired, this ballpark figure may be sufficient to direct your course. As you get closer to retirement, you should run the exercise again, perhaps once a year, striving for increasing accuracy. The better the numbers you put into this, the more valuable your results will be.

Your first task is to determine how much money you will need to live on during retirement. This is your base target. You want to find a figure that will cover your essential needs for food, clothing, shelter, and health care. Include your utilities and personal care and enough for a modest level of gifts, entertainment, and hobbies. Don't forget taxes.

You should be able to get a rough estimate of your needs from your current spending, with some modifications. (For example, after you're retired, you won't need to keep contributing to an IRA or a 401(k) plan. But you probably will pay more for medical care, possibly a lot more.)

The result will be an income estimate that could sustain you in retirement but not give you all the choices you'd like to have. Use today's dollars, without regard to inflation, an issue we'll address momentarily. This number is your base target.

Your second task is to estimate your live-it-up target. Start with the base target and add money for the optional but desirable things you want to do and have in retirement. These are discretionary expenses that you can cut if necessary. Travel, a second home, hobbies, and other activities are all part of this calculation.

How much desired income you add is totally subjective and up to you. Shoot for a level that seems very attractive, but not necessarily extravagant. For most people, a retirement income of $1 million a year (at least in today's dollars) is unrealistic and won't ever happen. You might like that idea, but that number won't be useful. If your live-it-up target is one and a half to two times the size of your base target, you're probably within the range of reality.

Here's how you'll use these two figures:

Your base target will determine whether and when you can afford to retire. Until you have enough assets (along with other sources of income) to give you this income, you'll need to keep accumulating savings. Your live-it-up target will tell you when it might be time to declare that enough is enough. If your assets are sufficient to achieve this level of income, you're in good shape to live the life to which you aspire. You can keep working past that point, of course, but you won't have to continue to save so aggressively. However, you will probably need to continue adding to your savings until the day you retire. The reason? Inflation.

We deal with inflation again in Chapter 13. Here, we're trying to get you into the ballpark. While you're accumulating assets, the way to account for inflation is to update your base target and your live-it-up target figures once a year. As you do that, you'll automatically adjust for higher prices for the things you spend money on. For example, if your overall expenses go up 5 percent, that will boost your base target. And, as we are about to see, that will automatically adjust the size of the portfolio you need.

To illustrate this next step, let's pick a couple of figures out of the blue and work with them. Assume you have determined that if you were to retire today, your base target annual income is $80,000 and that you desire a lifestyle that could be supported on $120,000 a year (your live-it-up target). This means that $80,000 becomes the all-important number.

The chances are excellent that you won't have to rely on your portfolio for the whole $80,000. You'll probably have Social Security; you may have a pension; and you might have other sources of income you can rely on such as annuity payments or rental income from real estate. You should have a relatively recent individual benefits estimate from the Social Security Administration that gives you a pretty good idea what to expect. If you aren't sure you trust Social Security and you want to be conservative, reduce that estimate by some percentage so you won't be in major trouble if those payments should dry up sometime in the future.

Add up all that nonportfolio expected income and convert it to an annual figure. In our example, let's assume all those payments add up to $30,000 a year. That leaves you with a gap of $50,000 that must come from your portfolio every year to meet your $80,000 base target income. The $120,000 live-it-up target leaves a gap of $90,000 to come from your portfolio.

At this point you can start to get a good handle on your retirement picture. You can see that your portfolio will have to provide at

least $50,000 a year of sustainable income, and that it would be nice
to have $90,000. If you can save enough that your portfolio can pro-
vide something between those numbers, you will be in the ballpark.

A quick-and-dirty rule of thumb is to multiply that yearly gap by 25.
The result tells you how big your portfolio should be on the day you
retire. That implies that you will withdraw 4 percent of the portfolio
for your first year. (As we shall see in Chapter 13, a carefully designed
portfolio can likely sustain that withdrawal rate for the rest of your
life, although there are no guarantees.)

In this example, if you were going to retire today, your portfolio
should be at least $1,250,000 (25 times $50,000). Ideally, it would
be worth $2,250,000 (25 times $90,000). With this calculation, suddenly your situation snaps into sharper focus. If you currently have
$1.5 million, you know that you're on track. If you're only a few
years away from your expected retirement date and your resources
are far short of what you think you'll need, you may have to work
longer, increase your savings, or change your lifestyle expectations
for retirement—or some combination of all three. If this is the case,
the sooner you find out about it, the more you can do about it.

Using a financial calculator or the help of an adviser, you can
apply this information to plan your savings rate or calculate the
time you'll be able to retire. For example, if you have accumulated
$900,000 and you want to retire in two years, you'd need to contrib-
ute very aggressively in order to have much chance of beating your
$1.25 million base target by much.

For another example, if you have $500,000 and you're adding
$20,000 a year, a financial calculator can tell you that steady annual
returns of 10 percent will take you to $1.25 million in about eight
years. Knowing that future market returns are uncertain and that
your living costs will probably go up (meaning you'll need more
than $1.25 million to retire), you might use that information to tar-
get a retirement date in 9 or 10 years.

If these calculations indicate a serious gap between what you can
save and what you'll need, that's a strong indication that you could
benefit from some professional financial help. (In Chapter 14, we
discuss how to find such help.)

Here are a few other things to keep in mind as you do your
calculations:

Try to avoid the common mistake of overestimating your expected
investment return. You'll probably want to become more conservative

as you get closer to retirement, blending more fixed-income funds with your equity funds. That will give you stability, but it will most likely also give you a lower return.

Emergencies and unwelcome life changes occur, often with significant expenses attached. When you're working, you can often recover from these things by redirecting your income, taking a second job, cutting back expenses, or even (although of course I don't recommend it) by reducing your savings for a while. But when you're retired, emergencies can turn into serious financial setbacks. Think about how you will deal with the risks of disability, death of a spouse or partner (which could reduce pension income), long-term care, and helping aging parents.

You can transfer some of those risks by buying insurance (and the premiums must become part of your budget). But the best plan may be a separate emergency fund. Therefore, consider whether you should increase the multiplier we used earlier (25 times your first-year retirement income) to 26 or 27.

You might want to add still a bit more, depending on your plans for the first year of your retirement. That first year is when many people have large one-time expenses such as buying a motor home or taking off for an extended trip. You'll need to make sure you can adequately fund any such first-year plans that you have. Be sure to discuss these issues with your spouse or partner, because both of you will be affected by the plans and choices you make. This is also a worthwhile topic to discuss with a financial planner, to make sure your plans and expectations are realistic.

I don't recommend shortcuts for estimating your expenses in retirement, but I know that many people take them. If you use your current income as the source for your base target, be wary of any formula that assumes you will need less money after you retire than before. That's not what usually happens.

Finally, you should figure out how you will measure your investment progress. In our society of conspicuous consumption, you may compare yourself (and your status in life) to your neighbors or your peers. If the neighbors have a new car or a new boat, should you have one too? The trouble is, your neighbors may be living the high life on borrowed money, building up a pile of debt that will come back to haunt them later. You probably don't know. Your neighbor may have inherited $800,000 and thus be able to afford lots of spending that you can't. You probably don't know.

Your neighbors' investment results are an equally lousy benchmark for you—even if you had that information. Your neighbor is unlikely to produce brokerage and mutual fund statements for you to look at. You'll be more likely to hear about the successes than the setbacks, and thus (assuming you care), you'll get an inaccurate picture of what is going on next door.

As we saw in Chapter 4, the U.S. stock market measured by an index such as the Standard & Poor's 500 Index is a lousy benchmark that could cause you to whine about very positive returns and brag about losing substantial amounts of money. In the end, the only benchmark that really matters is one you can now create for yourself: how you're doing in terms of meeting your own goals and needs.

If you follow the steps outlined in this chapter and repeat the analysis once a year or so, and if you adjust your base target and your live-it-up target accordingly, you'll be miles ahead of most people in knowing where you are and where you should be. You'll be ready to apply what you will learn in the next five chapters of this book: how to make your money do the most for you.

# CHAPTER 6

# Your Ideal Portfolio

*A workman who wants to do his work well must first sharpen his tools.*

—Confucius

Investors willing to give up chasing recent performance and trying to pick tomorrow's hottest managers can fall back on about 80 years of performance data. In this chapter we show how that data can be used to put together a world-class portfolio of low-cost mutual funds investing in asset classes that are likely to continue to outperform the Standard & Poor's 500 Index.

We recommend an investment program that is boringly predictable instead of dazzling and exciting. We call it "Your Ideal Portfolio," and we'll show you in this and the following chapters how to put it together. My goal, in a nutshell, is to give investors a piece of the action along with peace of mind. What investors need most is a strategy with enough power in good times to generate positive returns, coupled with enough protection in bad times to keep those investors from bailing out in discouragement.

This chapter looks in detail at the nature of diversification, noting the difference between real diversification and mere window dressing. The latter, unfortunately, is much too common in 401(k) plans and in many mutual funds.

**49**

As a point of reference, we look at how the pension funds of large U.S. companies have traditionally invested most of their money. We measure this model in terms of its risk and returns. This model is typically allocated 60 percent to stocks and 40 percent to bonds. Its returns are strong enough, and its risks tame enough, that it could meet the long-term needs of most investors. We see that the pension funds' strategy can be approximated using only two index funds.

Any investment strategy worthy of being called "ideal" must be held to a high standard. For our purposes, that means our goal is a plan that will provide higher returns and lower risks than the pension fund model, using no-load funds readily available to ordinary investors.

The key to making this work is smart equity diversification. The portfolio includes value stocks, growth stocks, real estate stocks, small stocks, and international stocks.

Your Ideal Portfolio will combine multiple asset classes, every one of which has higher risk than the S&P 500 Index. Yet when you combine them properly, their individual risks offset each other and produce a lower composite risk figure. The construction of Your Ideal Portfolio starts with an examination of the 40 percent fixed-income component in typical pension funds. Standard practice is to invest in long-term and intermediate-term corporate bonds. But we will see that investors can get a more favorable risk/reward combination by investing in government bond funds.

By the end of the chapter we will have built the foundation for putting together Your Ideal Portfolio.

With his permission, I begin this chapter by drawing on some of the work of my son, Jeff Merriman-Cohen, who is now the chief executive officer of the company I founded, Merriman Berkman Next. Jeff wrote an article that's available online at FundAdvice.com, my company's educational web site. The article is called "The perfect portfolio." Jeff and I, of course, understand that no "perfect" portfolio exists in real life. Any actual portfolio results from a series of decisions and choices that trade off various desired outcomes and undesired potential problems (risks, in other words).

In this chapter I borrow from Jeff's article because it does such a good job of reflecting a process we sometimes go through with new clients.

Before we dig in, I want to make sure you understand what I mean by calling what we're creating "Your Ideal Portfolio." I don't believe, and I don't mean to suggest, that any particular group of investments is ideal for every investor. Everybody's needs are different, and of course I can't know your individual situation as I write this book.

The word *Your* is crucial. I want you to wind up with the portfolio that is ideal for you and your circumstances. To facilitate that, I start by outlining what I believe is the ideal makeup of the two major components of a long-term portfolio—equity investments and fixed-income investments. That's the job of this and the next three chapters. Then (in Chapter 10) I show you how to find the proportions of these components that are just right for you.

Risk, as we saw in earlier chapters, is central to investing. In a bond, there are two main risks: maturity and credit. *Maturity risk* refers to the fact that rising interest rates tend to depress the prices of longer-term bonds more than shorter-term bonds. This makes long-term bonds riskier than short-term bonds. *Credit risk* refers to the fact that repayment is more reliable from a blue-chip company than from a company struggling to meet its obligations. And repayment is more reliable still from obligations of, or backed by, the U.S. government.

In any particular stock, there are many risks. But in the aggregate, as Jeff wrote so succinctly, stocks are more risky than bonds, smaller companies are more risky than large ones, and so-called value companies are riskier than growth companies. These risks are well-known, of course. Over long periods of time, stocks have outperformed bonds and, in the aggregate, value stocks and small-company stocks have offered investors higher returns than growth stocks and large-company stocks.

From 1927 through 2007, U.S. small-cap value stocks as a group produced an annualized return of 13.6 percent—or 3.2 percentage points above that of the S&P 500 Index. This asset class experienced a 12-year period, from 1975 through 1986, with no annual losses and cumulative gains of 2,148 percent, or about 29.6 percent annualized. Astonishing!

However, small-cap value stocks had 22 negative years from 1927 through 2002. Those losses averaged 18.3 percent. The biggest annual loss was 53.5 percent, part of a four-year losing streak with cumulative losses of about 85 percent. (That four-year streak, by the way, was immediately followed by a one-year gain of 142.5 percent. That looks mighty good on paper, but if you're down to 15 cents on the dollar of your original investment, a 142.5 percent gain brings you back up to only 36 cents.)

I discuss small-cap stocks and value stocks in later chapters. The question here is how investors can take advantage of asset classes like that without getting bruised and burned.

## How Reliable Are Stocks?

It's easy to see that stocks are more risky than fixed-income investments, and that much of the time they provide higher returns. But just how reliable is this premium return? And how long must an investor wait to be sure of getting it? Those are excellent questions. Investors who know the answers will have a real advantage over those who don't.

Investors have every reason to expect that stock investments will continue to provide premium returns over the long term. But over shorter periods, this won't always be the case. You should expect to see occasional multiyear periods when cash outperforms stocks (think of 2000 through 2002).

A study that included thousands of computer trials using actual market data from 1926 through 2007 gives some useful insight on the size and reliability of the equity market premium. The study, summarized in Table 6.1, compares the returns of the S&P 500 Index to that of no-risk Treasury bills.

To understand the table, start in the "1 Year" column. The figures were derived from studying every possible 12-month period (for example February 1967 through January 1968) from 1926 through 2007.

The numbers in the "Best," "Average," and "Worst" boxes are differences of return, expressed in percentage points. Here's how they work: In these 973 one-year periods, the average return from stocks was 8.9 percentage points higher than the corresponding return from T-bills. That means that if T-bills averaged 5 percent, stocks averaged 13.9 percent.

In the very best one-year period, if T-bills returned 5 percent, stocks returned 168 percent. In the worst period, stocks suffered a very sharp loss, equal to 68.9 percentage points below the return of T-bills.

The most important number is the bottom one, "Reliability." It indicates that in any 12 consecutive months, investors in equities had about two chances out of three of exceeding the return of T-bills. The other columns in the table show that the reliability factor increased until it reached 100 percent in periods of 20 years and longer.

**Table 6.1    Equity Premiums, 1926–2007**

| Period | 1 Year | 5 Years | 10 Years | 15 Years | 20 Years | 25 Years |
|---|---|---|---|---|---|---|
| Best | 162.6% | 35.9% | 19.7% | 18.0% | 15.7% | 15.4% |
| Average | 8.9% | 6.6% | 7.3% | 7.3% | 7.4% | 7.3% |
| Worst | −68.9% | −20.1% | −5.7% | −2.2% | 0.2% | 1.7% |
| Reliability | 69.0% | 77.2% | 86.1% | 94.5% | 100.0% | 100.0% |

The answer is smart diversification. When we meet with a client, we may pull out the chart that you see as Figure 6.1. It's called the "Theoretical Balance of Risk and Return 1970–2007." The graph looks very simple: a straight line! But in order to follow the upcoming discussion, you'll need to understand this graph.

This graph plots annual returns (in percentages, on the left) and levels of risk (in worst 12-month losses, along the bottom). Every point inside the graph represents a combination of a return and a level of risk. The area on the right side of the graph represents higher risks; the area on the left represents lower risks. Similarly, the area near the top represents higher returns, and the area near the bottom, represents lower returns. A theoretically perfect investment would be close to the upper left-hand corner of the graph, where risk is lowest and return is highest. We'll look at a series of graphs laid out this same way, always looking for combinations of assets that have more return and less risk.

In Figure 6.1, the top (right) end of the dotted line shows the risk and return of the S&P 500 Index from 1970 through 2007. The bottom (left) end of the line shows the risk and return of five-year Treasury notes. Just as you would expect, T-notes have much

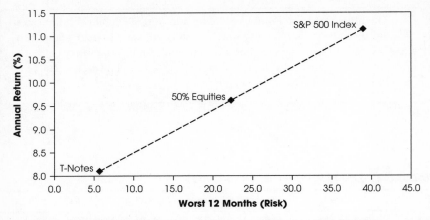

**Figure 6.1   Theoretical Balance of Risk and Return, 1970–2007**

less risk (and less return) than the S&P 500 Index. The point in the middle of the line shows what you might logically expect from a 50/50 combination of T-notes and the S&P 500 Index. This is the halfway point of both risk and return.

But in real life, it doesn't work out that way. You can see this in Figure 6.2, "Actual Balance of Risk and Return 1970–2007," which shows a solid line based on actual combinations of these two assets.

The solid line isn't straight. It's bent upward and toward the left. You can see that the actual 50/50 combination produced a

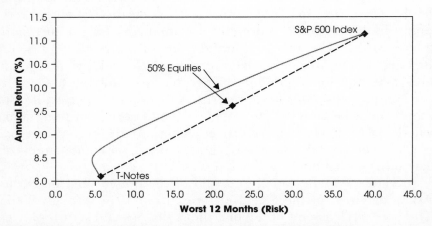

**Figure 6.2   Actual Balance of Risk and Return, 1970–2007**

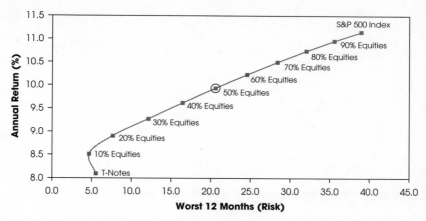

**Figure 6.3** **The Balance of Risk and Return, 1970-2007**

higher return than the average of the two individual returns, with lower risk.

Figure 6.3 adds some important information, showing where various percentage combinations of these two assets fall on this line. Every combination is higher than—and to the left of—where it would fall on the straight dotted line that we saw in Figure 6.1. One thing that pops out at me when I look at this graph is that the 20 percent equity combination has nearly a 10 percent higher return than T-notes alone—but with only minimal additional risk.

Think of the bend in that line as a benefit of diversification. As we will see, this phenomenon is not limited to these two particular assets. In fact, these three graphs show something very fundamental that savvy investors should understand: Smart diversification lets you mix two assets together and achieve a higher return, with less risk, than the average return of those two assets.

Choosing the right assets for this smart diversification is crucial, and in later chapters we discuss the most valuable ones and how to capture the premium returns they offer. But for right now, let's look further at smart diversification and why it works. Start with Figure 6.4. This shows a theoretical graph of return over some period of time of two investments, each of which starts with $100,000 and winds up being worth $200,000. Which one do you think is better?

Many of our clients have a tough time choosing between these, and for good reason. They are mirror images of each other, and

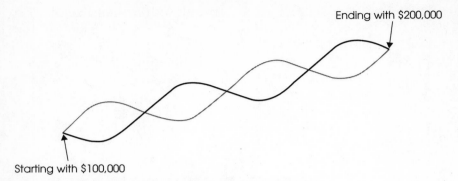

Ending with $200,000

Starting with $100,000

**Figure 6.4    Which Investment Would You Prefer?**

they wind up in the same place. (The only significant difference between them is that the investment that initially rises is less risky, in hindsight, than the one that initially falls, for the obvious reason that the former is never worth less than its initial cost.)

Now take a look at a graph called "Perfect Diversification," in Figure 6.5. The straight line up the middle represents the progress of a 50/50 combination of the two investments shown in Figure 6.4. These two theoretical assets have identical long-term rates of return. But in the shorter term, they are 100 percent negatively correlated: Each one does the exact opposite of the other.

Here's a critical point: Individually, each of these assets produces a good deal of angst in getting to its final result. But when they are

Ending with $200,000

Starting with $100,000

**Figure 6.5    Perfect Diversification**

put together, they achieve the same result with no angst at all. This is the key to making your money work hard for you while staying within your risk tolerance. Perfect diversification like this doesn't happen in real life, but it's a worthwhile direction in which to move when you're putting together a pool of investments that you hope will rise in value.

Here's a second crucial point: For diversification to work, it has to involve more than just owning different assets. They have to be assets that behave differently from each other.

This is why it doesn't do investors much good to hold several funds that behave similarly to the S&P 500 Index. Doing so may feel comfortable. But as one of my colleagues likes to say, three different brands of corn flakes may look different on the grocery store shelf, but what you get in the end is still just corn flakes.

The "just corn flakes" problem is more common than you might think. It turns out that many institutional investors fall into the same traps as individuals. Lots of 401(k) plans have multiple options that overlap each other and are focused mostly on large-cap U.S. stocks. It's not uncommon to find 401(k) plans that offer half a dozen such funds and perhaps a mid-cap stock fund, but nothing at all in the way of small-cap funds.

My company has examined scores of 401(k) and similar plans, and we've seen many (including one for employees of the U.S. government) that don't offer any value funds. It's extremely common for plans to have only one international fund. That's a real disservice to plan participants, as we will see later in this book. (You can find our analyses of individual plans, along with our recommendations for their participants, online at www.401khelp.com.) ✓

For the rest of this chapter, I want to concentrate on the fixed-income component of the typical pension fund portfolio. This makes up 40 percent of our ideal portfolio, and it's surprisingly easy to get it right. Whether your portfolio is heavy on bonds or light on bonds, it matters what kind of bonds you put into the mix. This is a simple but effective way to begin building Your Ideal Portfolio.

In general, longer bond maturities go together with higher yields and higher volatility, commonly measured by a statistic known as *standard deviation*. However, as you extend maturities beyond intermediate-term bonds, the added volatility (risk) rises much faster than the additional return.

In the past (including in the first edition of this book), we recommended short-term corporate bonds for this part of the portfolio. But after thorough study, we have refined our approach: The fixed-income part of the portfolio that we recommend is now exclusively in government funds. Half of it is made up of intermediate-term bond funds, 30 percent is in short-term bond funds, and 20 percent is in TIPS funds for inflation protection. (TIPS funds invest in U.S. Treasury inflation-protected securities, which automatically adjust their interest payments and their value to reflect changes in the Consumer Price Index.

For a variety of reasons, we expect this combination to produce slightly higher returns, with a little bit of additional risk. But because the added risk is in the form of longer-term bonds (instead of a greater risk of a corporate default), this extra risk is noncorrelated with the stock market. This is good. It means that when we combine this fixed-income mix with a diversified equity portfolio (which I'll explain in upcoming chapters), the volatility (risk, that is) of the whole portfolio goes down.

I know it's counterintuitive to think you can reduce risk by adding risk. But in this case, we believe it's quite possible. This is what I call smart diversification at work; we'll encounter this concept again in the equity side of the portfolio.

Why do we exclude corporate fixed-income funds? In a nutshell, we believe in taking calculated risks on the equity side of the portfolio while being very conservative on the fixed-income side.

At this point we come to the first two in a series of graphs that will help me show how to put together Your Ideal Portfolio. Figure 6.6 shows Portfolio 1, the standard pension fund portfolio. From 1970 through 2007, it achieved an annualized return of 10.2 percent, with a standard deviation of 11.2 percent. We're going to keep those numbers in mind and use them as a standard benchmark.

This return is not bad at all, especially considering that the period included three major bear markets. I believe that return should be more than enough to let most investors achieve their long-term goals. As we add asset classes and divide up the pie into more slices, our objective will be to increase the return while we decrease the risk. I won't go into the details of standard deviation here. For purposes of this discussion, the important thing to keep in mind is that lower standard deviation means lower risk because it describes a portfolio that's more predictable and less volatile.

| | Annualized Return | Annualized Standard Deviation |
|---|---|---|
| Portfolio One | 10.2% | 11.2% |

$100,000 grew to $4,066,109

40% Lehman Govt. Credit Index

## Modifying the Bond Portfolio

▶ Remove corporate bonds
▶ Reduce bond maturity
▶ Add inflation protection

**Figure 6.6   Portfolio 1, January 1970 – December 2007**

Hundreds of thousands (if not millions) of investors would be better off with this standard pension fund portfolio than they are with the investments they have, which typically combine inadequate diversification with unnecessarily high expenses and excessive risk. If those investors didn't do anything more than adopt Portfolio 1, which is easily duplicated using a few no-load index funds, they would be more likely to reach their goals and preserve their peace of mind.

Because of that, I believe this mix is a relatively high standard from which to begin. Anything worth being called an "ideal portfolio" must beat Portfolio 1 in both return and risk.

With the changes I have outlined regarding the 40 percent side of this portfolio, we can move immediately to Portfolio 2, shown in Figure 6.7.

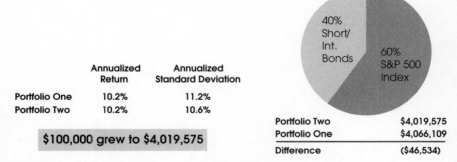

| | Annualized Return | Annualized Standard Deviation |
|---|---|---|
| Portfolio One | 10.2% | 11.2% |
| Portfolio Two | 10.2% | 10.6% |

$100,000 grew to $4,019,575

40% Short/ Int. Bonds

60% S&P 500 Index

| | |
|---|---|
| Portfolio Two | $4,019,575 |
| Portfolio One | $4,066,109 |
| Difference | ($46,534) |

**Figure 6.7   Portfolio 2, January 1970 – December 2007**

This portfolio had almost exactly the same return, 10.2 percent from 1970 through 2007, as Portfolio 1. Its standard deviation dropped to 10.6 percent. Though this is a small improvement, it is moving us in the right direction.

This is only the first step in creating the ideal combination of assets to let you retire in style. But even if you stopped here, this change would provide a smoother ride along the way. The move to government bonds gives more of what you want from bonds: stability. And it doesn't cost much in terms of performance.

This is a modest start. But stay tuned, because the best is yet to come.

# Profit from Real Estate and Small Companies

*Tall oaks from little acorns grow.*

—David Everett

If you want your retirement savings to work hard for you, there are four main changes you must make in the equity part of the standard pension fund's portfolio. The first is to add real estate companies. Another is to expand the asset mix to include stocks of smaller companies. A third is to include value companies that are out of favor. The fourth is to include international companies, those head-quartered outside the United States.

This chapter explores the first two of these changes. We'll see how real estate investment trusts (REITs) can add return and reduce risk. And we'll look at why small companies have historically produced bigger returns and how you can easily and efficiently capture them.

When most people think about owning real estate they think about owning their homes. But home ownership is sometimes overrated strictly as an investment. Commercial real estate is another matter. Adding a widely diversified portfolio of professionally managed residential and com-mercial properties can give a nice boost to an equity port-folio while reducing its risks.

The size effect—in other words, the benefit of owning smaller companies—is primarily a matter of potential. Investors looking for growth need to put their money where the growth potential lies, and one of those places is small companies. (Who's likely to grow more over the next year—a 13-year-old boy or a 27-year-old man?)

Compare two well-known companies with leading positions in important industries in the 1990s: IBM and Microsoft Corp. IBM sales grew from $69 billion in 1990 to $88 billion in 2000, a gain of 28 percent. Microsoft sales grew from $1.15 billion in 1990 to $23 billion in 2000, a gain of 1,896 percent. Shareholders who took the safer bet (in 1990) with IBM did well; that company's shares appreciated approximately 273 percent from mid-1990 to mid-2000. Microsoft, much smaller but hardly unknown in 1990, rewarded its shareholders with a gain of 3,689 percent in the same 10-year period. (Stock prices, supplied by Bloomberg L.P. and adjusted for splits, were measured from June 29, 1990 through June 30, 2000.)

The prudent way to benefit from small-company returns is not to invest in individual stocks but in small-company stocks as an asset class. (These are also known as small-cap stocks because the size of companies for this purpose is based on total market capitalization—the current stock price times the number of shares outstanding.) These returns can best be captured through mutual funds that invest in the whole asset class, not just a few small-cap stocks. Index funds are the most efficient vehicle for this.

Over long periods of time, small-cap stocks have outperformed large-cap ones. I expect this premium return to continue over the long haul. But in this case, the word *long* can really mean long! The effect can take decades to pay off, although investors whose timing is lucky can sometimes experience these gains quickly.

There are significant periods when small-cap stocks outperform, and vice versa. From 1994 through 2000, the largest U.S. stocks (large-cap) more than tripled in value, while the smallest 10 percent of stocks appreciated only about 80 percent. From 1975 through 1983, the largest 10 percent of U.S. stocks appreciated about 200 percent, while the smallest 10 percent gained about 1,300 percent. A series of dramatic charts in this chapter shows that size really does matter. The superior performance of small-cap stocks seems to persist in trends that last at least a few years. The same is true of large-cap stocks. But the charts also show that dramatic reversals can occur every few years, so it's not a good idea to invest exclusively in large-cap stocks or only in small-cap stocks.

There is no predictable pattern of how long these trends will last. In the seven time periods covered by our charts, small-cap stocks were king for periods of four to nine years. Large-cap stocks outperformed in periods that lasted from five to seven years.

As this is being written, small-cap stocks have outperformed in five of the most recent six years. But investors shouldn't get suckered into thinking that whichever trend is current is normal and will continue indefinitely. Instead, they should own both large-cap stocks and small-cap stocks in roughly equal amounts. And they should maintain this balance by annual rebalancing.

Virtually all investors are familiar with the long-term attraction of owning real estate. And I'll show you why I think it should be part of a well-diversified investment portfolio. If you think you have this asset class covered because you own your home, it is time to reevaluate that notion.

One of my colleagues bought a house in a Seattle suburb in 1978 for $70,000 and sold it 20 years later for $435,000. He thought this was terrific appreciation, and he was right—if all you look at is those two numbers. I asked him to figure out what his annual rate of return was on that house. It came out to about 9.6 percent. That's not bad at all. But the Standard & Poor's 500 Index compounded at 15.8 percent over those same 20 years. And a well-diversified portfolio like the one that we're building in this book did even better.

Of course, my colleague didn't buy that house as an investment. It was a place for his family to call home, and his gains on the sale were a welcome by-product that kept him well ahead of inflation.

Had he bought real estate the way I'm advocating for inclusion in Your Ideal Portfolio, he could have done much better purely in investment terms. To do that, he would have invested in mutual funds that own real estate investment trusts (REITs). These operate much like specialized mutual funds, each owning a portfolio of properties. The Dow Jones Wilshire REIT Index appreciated at the rate of 15.3 percent during that same 20-year period.

This index encompasses companies that build, own, and manage shopping centers, condominiums, office buildings, housing developments, hospitals, parking garages, and all sorts of other real estate that makes money.

From 1975 through 2007, REITs compounded at 15.3 percent, far outpacing the S&P 500 Index. This was an unusually productive period for REITs, and academic researchers expect the future returns of REITs and the S&P 500 Index to be much more similar to each other—though not as high as they were in this period.

The main point of adding REITs is not to improve return, though that would have happened in the past several decades. The point is to improve diversification. If you accept the premise that REITs and the S&P 500 Index will have similar returns in the future, why bother investing in both? Because they typically move up and down out of synch with each other.

As we saw in our discussion of perfect diversification in Chapter 6, that's a definite benefit. Your goal should be to improve diversification without sacrificing return, and REITs can help you do that.

From 1972 through 2007, there were many years when these two asset classes performed similarly—and many other years when their performance diverged. You can see the evidence in Table 7.1. You'll find 15 calendar years in which the return difference between these two asset classes was more than 20 percentage points. And if you look at the bear-market years 2000, 2001, and 2002, you'll see why I think it's worthwhile to substitute REITs for some of the S&P 500 Index in the original portfolio.

As you will see, when REITs make up one-fifth of the equity part of the portfolio we're building, the change boosts the annual return to 10.5 percent and drops the standard deviation (risk) to 9.9 percent. Over this long period of 38 years, the changes so far add $347,138 in cumulative return to the portfolio. You'll see this in Figure 7.1, depicting Portfolio 3.

This is a great start. But the best is yet to come.

Our next step is to take another 12 percent of the portfolio—another one-fifth of the equity part—away from the Standard & Poor's

**Table 7.1     REITs versus Standard & Poor's 500 Index, 1972–2007**

| Year | S&P 500 Index | REIT Index | Difference |
|------|--------------|-----------|-----------|
| 1972 | 19.0% | 7.7% | 11.3% |
| 1973 | −14.7% | −15.8% | 1.1% |
| 1974 | −26.5% | −21.7% | −4.8% |
| 1975 | 37.2% | 34.2% | 3.0% |
| 1976 | 23.8% | 38.7% | −14.9% |
| 1977 | −7.2% | 17.7% | −24.9% |
| 1978 | 6.6% | 11.0% | −4.4% |
| 1979 | 18.4% | 49.0% | −30.6% |
| 1980 | 32.4% | 33.1% | −0.7% |
| 1981 | −4.9% | 17.9% | −22.8% |
| 1982 | 21.4% | 20.9% | 0.5% |
| 1983 | 22.5% | 32.2% | −9.7% |
| 1984 | 6.3% | 21.9% | −15.6% |
| 1985 | 32.2% | 6.5% | 25.7% |
| 1986 | 18.5% | 19.7% | −1.2% |
| 1987 | 5.2% | −6.6% | 11.8% |
| 1988 | 16.8% | 17.5% | −0.7% |
| 1989 | 31.5% | 2.7% | 28.8% |
| 1990 | −3.1% | −23.4% | 20.3% |
| 1991 | 30.5% | 23.8% | 6.7% |
| 1992 | 7.6% | 15.1% | −7.5% |
| 1993 | 10.1% | 15.1% | −5.0% |
| 1994 | 1.3% | 2.7% | −1.4% |
| 1995 | 37.6% | 12.2% | 25.4% |
| 1996 | 23.0% | 37.0% | −14.0% |
| 1997 | 33.4% | 19.7% | 13.7% |
| 1998 | 28.6% | −17.0% | 45.6% |
| 1999 | 21.0% | −2.6% | 23.6% |
| 2000 | −9.1% | 31.0% | −40.1% |
| 2001 | −11.9% | 12.4% | −24.3% |
| 2002 | −22.1% | 3.6% | −25.7% |
| 2003 | 28.7% | 36.2% | −7.5% |
| 2004 | 10.9% | 33.2% | −22.3% |
| 2005 | 4.9% | 14.0% | −9.1% |
| 2006 | 15.8% | 36.1% | −20.3% |
| 2007 | 5.5% | −17.6% | 23.0% |

A real estate investment trust (REIT) fund invests in companies that own shopping malls, office buildings, apartments, warehouses, hotels, etc.

| 1975*-2007 | REITs | S&P 500 |
|---|---|---|
| Annualized Return | 15.3% | 13.3% |
| Annualized Standard Deviation | 16.8% | 15.5% |

|  | Annualized Return | Annualized Standard Deviation |
|---|---|---|
| Portfolio One | 10.2% | 11.2% |
| Portfolio Two | 10.2% | 10.6% |
| Portfolio Three | 10.5% | 9.9% |

**$100,000 grew to $4,413,247**

* REIT performance data only available over the time period of 1975–2007

12% REITs
40% Short/Int. Bonds
48% S&P 500 Index

| Portfolio Three | $4,413,247 |
|---|---|
| Portfolio One | $4,066,109 |
| Difference | $347,138 |

**Figure 7.1    Portfolio 3, January 1970 – December 2007**

500 Index and replace it with small U.S. companies. As we shall see, historically this significantly improves the long-term return while reducing volatility at the same time.

To make my point, I want to move right into the good stuff, by which I mean the evidence contained in seven charts, which we have reprinted with permission from Dimensional Fund Advisors. They cover the years 1965 through 2007, a 43-year period that's long enough to show you what you need to know about small and large companies.

Figure 7.2 shows the four years from 1965 through 1968, a period when small-cap stocks reigned supreme. The left-hand scale shows total return over this period. The bottom scale has 11 positions, 10 of which represent the U.S. stock market as if it were sliced into 10 deciles.

To understand these, imagine that you had a list of all publicly traded stocks ranked by market capitalization (current stock price times outstanding shares). The 10 percent of names at the bottom of your list represent the tenth decile, the smallest U.S. companies you can invest in. The next 10 percent of names represent the ninth decile, and so forth, with the first decile representing the very largest companies.

The second bar in Figure 7.2 represents the S&P 500 Index, which is dominated by large, familiar U.S. companies like Wells Fargo, Procter & Gamble, Wal-Mart, Pfizer, Citigroup, and Cisco. Each of these, by the way, was once a small company going through rapid growth that paid off in a big way for early investors.

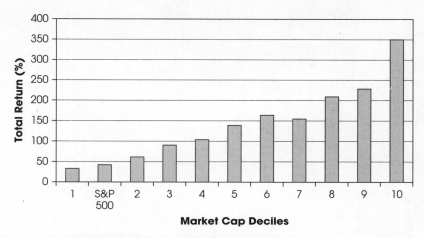

**Figure 7.2    Impact of Company Size, 1965–1968**

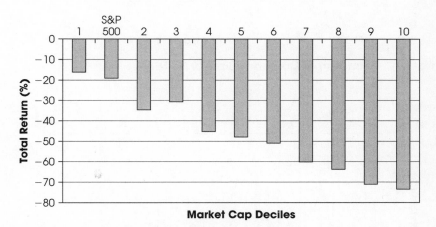

**Figure 7.3    Impact of Company Size, 1969–1974**

Figure 7.2 makes it clear that the size effect—smaller companies outperforming larger ones—apparently isn't random. All the way up and down that scale, smaller companies do better.

Figure 7.3, covering a period when stocks were declining, shows a strong reversal. In those years, the largest companies held up much better. Again, the size effect is unmistakable. Another reversal occurred in 1975, and small-company stocks once again took over the leadership for nine years, as you can see in Figure 7.4.

By the early 1980s, many investors had concluded that small-cap companies were the ones that paid off. Imagine their surprise from 1984 through 1990, when (as you can see in Figure 7.5) large-cap

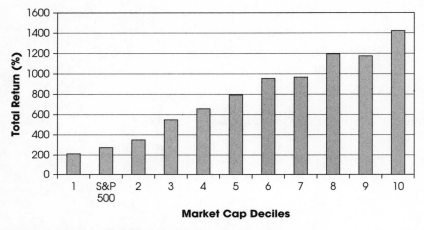

**Figure 7.4   Impact of Company Size, 1975–1983**

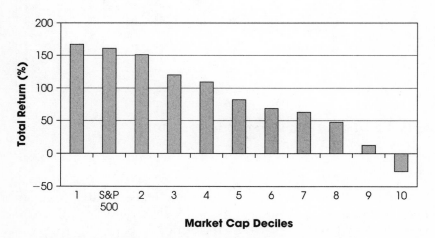

**Figure 7.5   Impact of Company Size, 1984–1990**

stocks dwarfed the returns of small ones. The four-year period from 1991 through 1993 (Figure 7.6) indicates another reversal, followed by the five years shown in Figure 7.7, when large-cap stocks led the way once again. Figure 7.8 shows still another period of small-cap supremacy from 1999 through 2007.

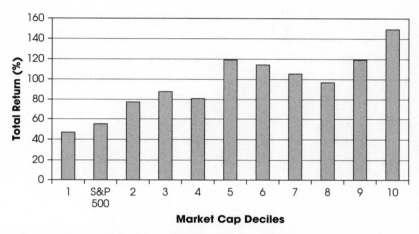

**Figure 7.6   Impact of Company Size, 1991–1993**

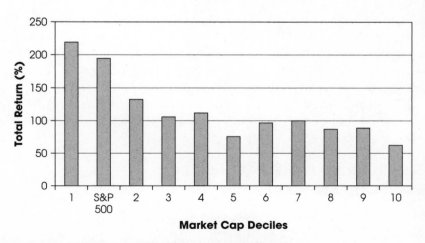

**Figure 7.7   Impact of Company Size, 1994–1998**

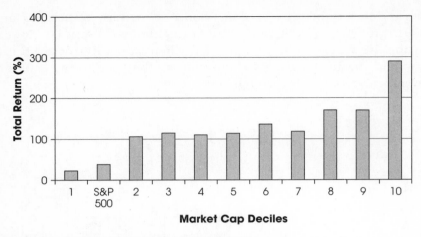

**Figure 7.8**    **Annualized Returns, 1999–2007**

It's not hard to see that over periods of several years or more, small-cap stocks and large-cap stocks go sharply in and out of favor among investors. Rarely have both groups been extremely productive or extremely unproductive at the same time.

Over much longer periods, small-cap stocks have shown a distinct advantage. From 1927 through 2007, small-cap U.S. stocks produced an annualized return of 11.8 percent, versus 10.4 percent for the S&P 500 Index. That difference of 1.4 percentage points might seem trivial, but it's not. Over a period of 40 years, which is well within the potential investment lifetime of most investors, an initial investment of $10,000 compounding at 10.4 percent (large-cap U.S. stocks) grows to $523,315. But if it compounded at 11.8 percent over 40 years, the same $10,000 would grow to $866,308—an increase of more than 65 percent.

## How Reliable Is the Premium from Small-Cap Stocks?

A study of 82 years of market history shows that the premium return from owning stocks of small-cap companies (as opposed to large-cap companies) is considerably more likely to show up over long periods than in shorter ones.

The data are summarized in Table 7.2, which is identical in format to Table 6.1, presented and explained in Chapter 6. This table shows that in periods of 12 months, small-cap stocks had an average advantage of 6.6 percentage points over large-cap stocks. But as the bottom figure in the "1 Year" column shows, only 53 percent of these 12-month periods gave investors any premium return for investing in small-cap stocks. This premium became more reliable in periods lasting 10 years or more.

However, the figures also indicate that investors who rely totally on small-cap stocks could fall behind even in a 25-year period. This is why we recommend that investors include large-cap stocks in their portfolios as well as small-cap stocks.

Small-cap investing works internationally, too, although reliable data aren't available for years before 1970. From 1970 through 2007, small-cap international companies compounded at 16.1 percent. That compares with 10.7 percent for large-cap international companies.

Table 7.3 lists year-by-year results for large-cap U.S. stocks (the S&P 500 Index), small-cap U.S. stocks, large-cap international stocks (Morgan Stanley Europe Australia Far East Index known as EAFE), and small-cap international stocks. The final column shows the results of combining all four with equal weighting.

At the bottom of each column are three cumulative figures that apply to the whole period: compound rate of return (CRR); the results of an initial $10,000 left to grow; and standard deviation, a measure of risk. (The most important thing to know about standard deviation is that smaller numbers indicate less risk.)

Small-cap investing has been productive. But it hasn't been easy. In the extended periods when small-cap stocks fall behind larger ones, investors can easily lose faith. That's why it's useful to remember why small-cap stocks tend to outperform over long periods.

**Table 7.2   Small-Cap Equity Premiums, 1926–2007**

| Period | 1 Year | 5 Years | 10 Years | 15 Years | 20 Years | 25 Years |
|---|---|---|---|---|---|---|
| Best | 392.1% | 44.9% | 16.5% | 17.7% | 11.8% | 8.5% |
| Average | 6.6% | 3.4% | 2.9% | 2.8% | 2.7% | 2.6% |
| Worst | −62.7% | −23.3% | −7.3% | −7.5% | −3.5% | −1.7% |
| Reliability | 53.0% | 56.0% | 63.7% | 72.0% | 78.4% | 89.2% |

**Table 7.3 Small Cap versus Large Cap Stocks U.S. and International**

| Year | US Large Companies | US Small Companies | Int'l Large Companies | Int'l Small Companies | Combined |
|------|------|------|------|------|------|
| 1970 | 3.9 | −18.2 | −11.9 | 0.3 | −6.1 |
| 1971 | 14.1 | 17.9 | 29.2 | 67.4 | 31.4 |
| 1972 | 18.8 | −0.1 | 36.0 | 63.3 | 27.9 |
| 1973 | −14.8 | −38.6 | −15.2 | −14.2 | −20.8 |
| 1974 | −26.6 | −26.7 | −23.4 | −29.0 | −25.8 |
| 1975 | 37.0 | 57.8 | 35.0 | 49.0 | 45.2 |
| 1976 | 23.7 | 48.2 | 2.2 | 10.8 | 20.5 |
| 1977 | −7.3 | 25.7 | 17.7 | 73.1 | 24.9 |
| 1978 | 6.4 | 24.7 | 32.3 | 64.6 | 32.2 |
| 1979 | 18.2 | 42.0 | 4.5 | −1.3 | 15.0 |
| 1980 | 32.2 | 39.1 | 22.2 | 34.7 | 32.6 |
| 1981 | −5.1 | −2.2 | −2.6 | −5.2 | −3.3 |
| 1982 | 21.2 | 27.2 | −2.1 | 0.3 | 11.4 |
| 1983 | 22.3 | 39.7 | 23.3 | 31.7 | 29.4 |
| 1984 | 6.1 | −6.7 | 7.1 | 9.5 | 4.1 |
| 1985 | 32.0 | 24.7 | 55.7 | 59.2 | 42.8 |
| 1986 | 18.3 | 6.9 | 69.0 | 49.3 | 34.7 |
| 1987 | 5.1 | −9.3 | 24.3 | 69.6 | 20.1 |
| 1988 | 16.6 | 22.9 | 27.9 | 25.3 | 23.7 |
| 1989 | 31.3 | 10.2 | 10.2 | 28.6 | 20.1 |
| 1990 | −3.3 | −21.6 | −23.7 | −17.2 | −15.9 |
| 1991 | 30.1 | 44.6 | 15.7 | 6.5 | 23.9 |
| 1992 | 7.3 | 23.3 | −13.1 | −18.8 | −1.0 |
| 1993 | 9.6 | 21.0 | 25.9 | 32.8 | 22.5 |
| 1994 | 1.3 | 3.1 | 5.3 | 11.8 | 5.4 |
| 1995 | 37.1 | 34.5 | 13.0 | −0.1 | 20.4 |
| 1996 | 22.6 | 17.6 | 6.3 | 2.1 | 12.2 |
| 1997 | 33.1 | 22.8 | 5.5 | −23.7 | 7.8 |
| 1998 | 28.7 | −7.3 | 18.2 | 8.2 | 11.6 |
| 1999 | 20.8 | 29.8 | 28.5 | 21.9 | 25.7 |
| 2000 | −9.3 | −3.6 | −14.0 | −5.4 | −7.1 |
| 2001 | −12.1 | 22.8 | −20.8 | −10.5 | −6.0 |
| 2002 | −22.2 | −13.3 | −14.6 | 1.9 | −12.1 |
| 2003 | 28.5 | 60.7 | 36.7 | 58.8 | 45.7 |
| 2004 | 10.7 | 18.4 | 18.8 | 30.9 | 19.6 |
| 2005 | 4.9 | 5.7 | 13.5 | 22.0 | 11.5 |
| 2006 | 15.7 | 16.2 | 24.9 | 24.9 | 20.4 |
| 2007 | 5.4 | −5.2 | 12.5 | 5.7 | 4.5 |

| Year | US Large Companies | US Small Companies | Int'l Large Companies | Int'l Small Companies | Combined |
|---|---|---|---|---|---|
| Compound Rate of Return | 10.9 | 12.1 | 10.7 | 16.1 | 13.0 |
| Growth of $10,000 | $508,585 | $771,162 | $472,621 | $2,928,546 | $1,042,987 |
| Standard Deviation | 15.1 | 20.9 | 16.2 | 17.4 | 14.2 |
| Worst Month | −21.5 | −29.2 | −14.5 | −12.6 | −18.6 |
| Worst 3 Months | −29.6 | −32.6 | −21.3 | −24.3 | −21.9 |
| Worst 12 Months | −39.0 | −39.4 | −38.4 | −41.7 | −37.3 |
| Worst 36 Months | −41.2 | −55.1 | −46.1 | −28.5 | −31.1 |
| Worst 60 Months | −18.0 | −56.6 | −28.2 | −19.9 | −9.6 |

In general, investors get paid for taking risks, especially for taking prudent risks. As you can see from the standard deviation line in Table 7.3, small-cap stocks can be riskier than large-cap ones.

Small-cap stocks are riskier because they are newer companies, typically with fewer products, less depth of management, and higher costs of capital. And of course they don't have long, reassuring track records.

A large, mature company has already proven it can survive competition and weather economic storms. An upstart can fall on its face, and many do. Smaller companies can produce better returns because they can grow faster. I don't see any reason to think this basic relationship will change. I believe small companies will continue to be riskier than large ones. I believe that over time, investors in small companies will continue to be rewarded for taking those higher risks. But over shorter periods, I believe small-cap investing will continue to be challenging because of periods like those shown in Figures 7.3, 7.5, and 7.7, when large-cap stocks did much better than small-cap ones.

The answer is to invest in both small-cap and large-cap stocks—and to rebalance every year. This annual rebalancing keeps the risk of this combination in check. And it forces you to take some profits each year from whichever size category, large or small, has outperformed and then put those profits into the underperforming category. (Hint: This is called buying low and selling high. It's something that successful investors do.)

The right-hand column of Table 7.3 shows the hypothetical returns from 1970 through 2007 of putting all four of these asset classes together and rebalancing them every year. As you can see, the balanced (and rebalanced) portfolio would have been less risky than a portfolio made up of any one of the four components. And its cumulative return beat three of those four components.

Figure 7.9 is modeled on some of the graphs we introduced in Chapter 6. As you can see, for the period in the study, U.S. small-cap stocks were significantly more productive and also significantly more risky than large-cap stocks. But the curved line on the chart also shows that a 50/50 combination provided more return, at less risk, than the average of the two, which would fall on the midpoint of a straight line connecting the two ends of the curve. It's another example of what I call smart diversification.

We're now ready to take the next step in building Your Ideal Portfolio by shifting 12 percent of the pie from the S&P 500 Index into small-cap U.S. stocks. To represent small-cap stocks we use the

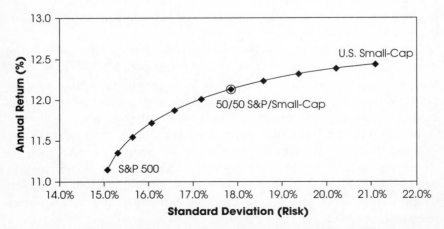

**Figure 7.9   The Balance of S&P 500 versus U.S. Small-Cap Stocks, 1970–2007**

|  | Annualized Return | Annualized Standard Deviation |
|---|---|---|
| Portfolio One | 10.2% | 11.2% |
| Portfolio Two | 10.2% | 10.6% |
| Portfolio Three | 10.5% | 9.9% |
| Portfolio Four | 10.7% | 10.2% |

**$100,000 grew to $4,784,522**

| | |
|---|---|
| Portfolio Four | $4,784,522 |
| Portfolio One | $4,066,109 |
| Difference | $718,413 |

**Figure 7.10    Portfolio 4, January 1970 – December 2007**

results of the Dimensional Fund Advisors U.S. Micro Cap Fund, which invests in the 9th and 10th deciles of the U.S. stock market.

The result is presented in Figure 7.10, called Portfolio 4. This step adds 0.2 percentage points to the return of Portfolio 3. At the same time, its standard deviation has increased slightly.

This means we have more work ahead to achieve our goal of a higher return at lower risk. We'll get to that work in the next two chapters.

At this point, it's worth noting that the changes we have made so far have added $718,413 to the long-term results of the standard pension fund, with a one-percentage-point decrease in risk.

# CHAPTER 8

# Value

## OWNING WHAT OTHERS DON'T WANT

*The word* crisis *in Chinese is composed of two characters. The first is the symbol of danger, the second the symbol of opportunity.*
—Unknown

One of the most fundamental mistakes investors make is paying high prices for popular assets. The message of this chapter is that you should invest in stocks that other investors don't want, stocks whose prices may have been going down instead of up.

It's a pity more investors don't behave like good shoppers. If they did, they'd look for opportunities to snap up good assets when they're on sale. The good news is that an important part of what investors need is always on sale.

According to the strange logic followed by so many investors, it's apparently better to pay full price for stocks, or even pay more than full price, when everybody else wants them, instead of buying them when they're on sale. This is one of the main reasons so many investors found themselves in deep trouble in 2000, 2001, and 2002. Back in the late 1990s, they bought technology and telecommunications stocks as if the prices they paid didn't matter.

To oversimplify somewhat, you can say the universe of stocks is divided into two parts: growth stocks and value stocks. When they are owned properly, value stocks pay more than growth stocks. Growth stocks represent excellent companies that inspire pride and hope. These companies tend to have good management, good products, strong financial positions, rising sales, rising profits, and rising prospects. Not coincidentally, they often have rising stock prices, too. Value stocks represent companies that are unexcellent and unpopular for any number of reasons. They may be in dead-end industries. They may have made big mistakes. They may be saddled with terrific competition, crummy management, and obsolete products.

So what's not to like about growth companies? The companies themselves are often wonderful. So wonderful that investors have bid their stock prices up to levels at which Wall Street must expect—and even demand—that these companies keep churning out nearly miraculous results. One slip, and billions of dollars of stock market value can be wiped out in a few minutes.

And what's good about value stocks? The one thing you can say about them for sure is that they are cheap. They let investors buy low, a critical (and often overlooked) part of the time-tested formula: Buy low, sell high.

Am I saying you should buy some dog stocks and pay for them by selling popular stocks like (at least in 2008) Google and Apple? Not at all. Smart investors don't buy value stocks one by one. There are almost always valid reasons why any particular value stock is out of favor. The best way to buy value stocks is by the thousands, through mutual funds that specialize in them. Buy the whole asset class, and you won't need to lose sleep when a handful of these companies bite the dust.

The folks on Wall Street are by no means stupid, and a portfolio full of value stocks will inevitably contain plenty of dogs. If you make a list of today's top value stocks, after five years you'll probably find at least half of those stocks still on the list (and some will be out of business). If you buy only a handful of value stocks, you could easily wind up entirely invested in companies that deserve permanent "value" status, and in that case you won't get the premium return you expect for investing in value companies. But if you buy the whole asset class and hold it long enough, you'll likely be glad you did. Over the years, a large group of value stocks has a very high likelihood of outperforming an equally large group of popular growth stocks.

Why is this true? It comes back to the basic formula of how investing works. Investors get paid for taking risks. Value stocks are more risky than more popular growth stocks. Fortunately, mutual funds that invest in value stocks give investors a way to cash in on the gains while mitigating most of the risks.

Virtually all the famous investment managers of the past 50 years (Warren Buffett, Peter Lynch, Ben Graham, Bill Miller, Michael Price, John Templeton) made their marks by investing in value stocks. Shouldn't you pay attention to their examples?

If you don't believe in the concept of buying low and selling high, it's pretty hard to know what you should do instead. But if you do believe in buying low and selling high, then you'll have to be willing to take opportunities to buy assets when their prices are low. When prices are declining and nobody seems to want that asset, it takes a strong leap of faith to buy it. This faith, when it's based on knowledge of the past, is one thing that separates successful investors from frustrated ones.

Identifying small-cap stocks is pretty easy. But identifying value stocks is trickier, because there are many ways to measure value. The basic point is that value stocks are bargains. Bargain investments are often measured subjectively by estimating their future values; investors then believe a stock is a good buy if it's likely it will return to its normal level when investors come to their senses. I don't like to rely on human judgment that much, and fortunately that isn't necessary. Investors can get the benefits of value investing by adopting a mechanical method for identifying value stocks.

This mechanical approach starts by identifying the largest 50 percent of stocks traded on the New York Stock Exchange and all other public companies of similar size, based on their market capitalization. The companies are then sorted by the ratio of their price per share to their book value per share. (*Book value* represents the total value of a company's assets on its balance sheet. In a rough way, it values the business not as a going concern but as a collection of assets that could be sold at an industrial garage sale.)

The top 30 percent of stocks on this list, those with the highest price-to-book ratios, are classified as growth companies. The theory is that they are valued by investors more for their future profitability than for the assets they own. The bottom 30 percent of stocks on the list are classified as value companies.

Although growth stocks are the most popular ones (and almost universally regarded as the safest investments), much research shows that historically, unpopular (value) stocks outperform popular (growth) ones.

To give you the numbers, I'll turn to the best academic research I'm aware of, studies by Dr. Eugene Fama of the University of Chicago and Dr. Kenneth French of Yale:

- Among U.S. large-company stocks, from 1927 through 2007, growth stocks had an annualized total return of 7.9 percent; value stocks grew at a rate of 11.4 percent. What does that mean in real terms? Over a 40-year period, it's the difference between turning an initial investment of $10,000 into $209,343 (growth stocks) or $750,598 (value stocks).
- Among U.S. small-company issues from 1927 through 2007, growth stocks grew at 8.6 percent, value stocks at 13.5 percent. That's the difference over a 40-year period between turning $10,000 into $271,140 (growth stocks) or into $1,584,289 (value stocks). The academics say this same relationship has been found time after time virtually everywhere in the world. The one exception is in Italy; the researchers haven't figured out why that country is an anomaly.
- Value stocks have another terrific attribute: They behave differently from growth stocks. You can see this clearly in Figure 8.1, which compares returns from the S&P 500 Index with those of large-cap value stocks from 1970 through 2007. The 50/50 combination we recommend, as you can see, adds about 1.5 percentage points of return to the S&P 500 Index while reducing risk nicely from the large value index.

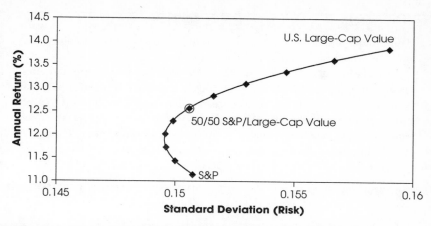

**Figure 8.1   The Balance of S&P 500 versus U.S. Large-Cap Value Stocks, 1970–2007**

Of course, not all value companies will turn out to be worth owning. When you go shopping, you know that not everything with a low price is a true bargain. Many stock analysts spend virtually all their time trying to figure out which stocks are underpriced and which aren't; most of those analysts fail to continually and repeatedly beat the indexes. Even full-time professionals make plenty of mistakes, and you're likely to do the same if you try this on your own. Unless you're a professional, the best way to buy value stocks is to buy lots of them, through index funds.

## How Reliable Are Value Stocks?

In each of the previous two chapters, we cited a study of many years of market history and presented partial results in figures like Table 8.1. This table focuses on the premium return investors may expect from value stocks when compared with growth stocks. The meaning of this data is explained in Chapter 6.

Table 8.1 shows that in periods of a single year, value stocks had an average advantage of 5.5 percentage points over growth stocks. And while some premium occurred in about 65 percent of the possible one-year periods,

*(Continued)*

value stocks were sometimes far, far behind—as you can see from the worst 12-month period, in which value stocks returned about 48 percentage points less than growth stocks.

We saw in earlier chapters that longer periods produced larger and more reliable premium returns from investing in equities instead of T-bills and from investing in small-cap stocks instead of large-cap ones. Table 8.1 shows that the same held true with value stocks. As you can see in the "15 years" column, as long as you held value stocks for at least 15 years, about 95 percent of the time you would have achieved a higher return. And the premium was almost certain with a 20-year holding period.

**Table 8.1   Value Premiums, 1926–2007**

| Period | 1 Year | 5 Years | 10 Years | 15 Years | 20 Years | 25 Years |
|---|---|---|---|---|---|---|
| Best | 130.4% | 20.7% | 12.5% | 10.1% | 8.5% | 8.3% |
| Average | 5.5% | 4.9% | 5.0% | 5.2% | 5.4% | 5.5% |
| Worst | −47.9% | −12.8% | −7.5% | −3.7% | 0.0% | 1.2% |
| Reliability | 64.9% | 81.8% | 89.4% | 94.2% | 100.0% | 100.0% |

Incidentally, value investing works with international stocks, too, although the data doesn't go back quite as far as for U.S. stocks. From 1975 through 2007, an index of international value stocks appreciated at an annual rate of 17.5 percent. By contrast, an index of large-company international stocks (mostly growth companies) rose at a rate of 10.7 percent.

In short, if you're looking for long-term results above those that come from following the crowd, you're likely to find them from owning value stocks.

The next step in building Your Ideal Portfolio is shown in Figure 8.2, called Portfolio 5. To take this step, we split the equity side of the pie into five slices instead of three, adding U.S. large value stocks and U.S. small value stocks. This boosts the annualized return of the portfolio to 11.6 percent, while reducing the standard deviation to 11.0 percent.

|  | Annualized Return | Annualized Standard Deviation |
|---|---|---|
| Portfolio One | 10.2% | 11.2% |
| Portfolio Two | 10.2% | 10.6% |
| Portfolio Three | 10.5% | 9.9% |
| Portfolio Four | 10.7% | 10.2% |
| Portfolio Five | 11.6% | 11.0% |

**$100,000 grew to $6,451,766**

| Portfolio Five | $6,451,766 |
|---|---|
| Portfolio One | $4,066,109 |
| Difference | $2,385,657 |

**Figure 8.2    Portfolio 5, January 1970 – December 2007**

This is an extremely significant improvement, because we have achieved a return that's 13.7 percent higher than our starting point while reducing volatility slightly.

Some investors might be quite content to stop here. But there's one more very important step in creating Your Ideal Portfolio. We discuss it in the next chapter.

CHAPTER

# Putting the World to Work for You

*In investing, what is comfortable is rarely profitable.*
—Robert Arnott

A recurring piece of nonsense that is taught to many investors is that they can get all the investment performance they'll ever need or want from companies based in the United States. The reality is that less than half of the world's stock market value resides in companies based in the United States. The rest is beyond the U.S. borders. Throughout this book, I urge investors to diversify. That's the most fundamental piece of investment advice I know. I believe almost all investors should have some exposure to international stocks.

The stocks of companies with headquarters outside the United States don't always outperform those of U.S. companies. But there are years—and multiyear periods—in which U.S. stocks take a back seat to international ones. That's why I counsel investors, including my company's clients, to have half their equity investments in international funds.

One of the biggest risks investors take is believing too strongly that they know what they are doing—overconfidence, if you will. Investors in Japan in 1990 had every legitimate reason to believe that they didn't need to invest in stocks outside their own country, which at the time seemed to be on the brink of having the world's largest economy.

Nobody could have credibly predicted that the bottom would fall out of the Japanese market for the next dozen or more years. Yet that's exactly what happened. Japanese investors whose capital was tied up exclusively in their own country's stocks paid a terrible price. Coming from the lips of an adviser or an investor, "It can't happen here" is an invitation for trouble.

Even if international stocks do not outperform their U.S. counterparts, they provide a frequently overlooked but intensely valuable diversification benefit to retirees who are regularly taking money from their portfolios. In fact, as we shall see, international stocks can make the difference between a retirement portfolio that lasts a lifetime and one that runs out of money prematurely.

Adding international stocks to Your Ideal Portfolio finishes the job of creating an investment combination with higher returns and lower risks than the standard pension fund model.

I've been asked why I recommend splitting the equity part of a portfolio equally between U.S. and international stocks. The answer is simplicity itself: because it works, for many legitimate reasons.

Many people are wary of investing outside the United States, partly from fear of the unknown. Some investment gurus have found a ready audience for the idea that investors can fully participate in the global economy if they own shares of large U.S.–based multinational companies that do a great deal of their business overseas. Prominent examples are Coca-Cola, Microsoft, and McDonald's.

It's true that international business is extremely important to these companies. But anybody who owns an S&P 500 Index fund has plenty of exposure to companies like that. Owning more of them, in the name of international investing, is really little more than piling on more large-cap U.S. growth stocks.

We will see in this chapter that over long periods of time (and in many short periods as well), international stocks have outperformed U.S. stocks. But you shouldn't include them in your portfolio primarily for a premium return. You should include them in your portfolio because they reduce risk when they're combined with U.S. stocks.

Now of course I know that investing internationally makes a lot of people skittish. And I know you will make up your own mind what to do. However, before you dismiss the idea out of hand, I hope you'll join me while we examine the most obvious risk of owning an equity portfolio based exclusively in the United States.

In the late 1980s and the early 1990s, it was obvious to anybody who read the newspapers that Japan was on a meteoric economic rise. Japan's economy, the second largest in the world, seemed to be on the brink of threatening the United States for the number one position. Many Japanese tourists had buckets of money to spend in North America. Japanese money propped up the sale of U.S. Treasury securities.

Many people were startled when Japanese interests purchased an American icon in New York City, Rockefeller Center. Some developers predicted that U.S. business parks specializing in technology companies would soon be accessible by freeway exit ramps with Japanese names like "Fuji Boulevard." Some of their predictions may seem silly today, but they were credible at the time.

Now imagine that you were an investor working and living in Japan in 1990. If you were prudent, you might have thought about buying stocks in large U.S. companies. But you probably would have been scoffed at. You might have been told something like this: "There's no need to invest outside Japan; everything you need is right here, and we are leading the world."

While that may have sounded credible, an unfortunate thing happened on the way to this promised nirvana: It didn't pan out. The Japanese Nikkei index started falling, on its way from 38,916 yen in December 1989 to a low of 7,752 yen in April 2003. Japan had a thriving mutual fund industry, but 90 percent of that industry's assets disappeared in losses and redemptions. While Japanese stocks went into this major spiral throughout the 1990s, the U.S. stock market had one of its best decades ever.

The numbers: From 1990 through 2006, large-company stocks in Japan (including such traditionally safe companies as Sony, Toyota, and Mitsubishi) had a negative annual compound return of 0.8 percent. That's a figure that has a minus sign in front of it, and it's compounded over 17 years. That rate of return is equivalent to reducing a $1,000 investment to just $872—if anybody had hung in there for 17 years. Think of the shattered dreams that loss represents. Remember, that resulted from investing in large Japanese companies that were seen as very safe. Small-company Japanese stocks in the same 17 years had a negative annualized return of 1.3 percent, a rate that would have reduced $1,000 to $801. Imagine how this would have felt to a Japanese retiree who was depending on Japanese equity funds.

So I am now giving the same counsel to you, presumably a U.S.-based investor, that millions of Japanese investors must wish they had heeded in 1990: No matter how high your confidence level is, don't invest all your money in your own country.

The key question is how much international exposure an investor should have. Based on extensive study of this issue, for more than a dozen years we have been recommending half-and-half as an excellent choice for most investors. By splitting your equities equally between U.S. and international funds, you essentially say, "Why choose?"

## Investing in Global and Worldwide Funds

Many mutual fund companies manage funds that include both U.S. and international stocks, hoping to attract investors who want a one-fund package to give them all they need.

Unfortunately, such funds aren't a good substitute for international funds. Typically, global and worldwide funds have a significant minority—and sometimes it's the majority—of their portfolios in U.S.-based stocks.

The giant American Funds New Perspective Fund (ANWPX) has 28 percent of its assets in U.S. stocks. Fidelity Worldwide Fund (FWWFX) has 43 percent of its portfolio in U.S. stocks. For Janus Worldwide Fund (JAWWX) it's 50 percent, and for Dreyfus Premier Worldwide Growth Fund (DPWRX), 52 percent.

We looked at 10 of the largest funds in Morningstar's "world stock" category and found that on average, they kept 42 percent of their assets in U.S. equities. This makes them a lousy substitute for the international funds that we recommend. In addition, such funds are usually filled primarily with large growth-oriented companies. That further detracts from proper diversification.

In our view, the best advice regarding worldwide and global stock funds is to "just say no."

How did we come to that conclusion? It was simple: We used the lessons of the past as our best guide. We have reliable data back to the 1950s for international stocks, giving us a window into history that's large enough to see long-term patterns. Almost all investors go through two distinct phases: accumulation and withdrawal. International stocks contribute to the results in each one, but in different ways, so we'll examine them separately.

Table 9.1 shows year-by-year returns starting in January 1970 for two all-equity portfolios. The first portfolio had no international funds; the second was made up of half U.S. funds and half international funds.

In Table 9.2, we show the bottom-line results of these two portfolios for 38 years, from 1970 through 2007. As you can see, an initial investment of $10,000 in the all-U.S. portfolio grew to $774,684 by the end of 2007, while the same investment in the portfolio with equal parts of U.S. and international equities grew to $1,335,529. The superiority of the more diversified portfolio established itself quickly and never faded.

After just two years, at the end of 1971, the globally diversified portfolio was worth $12,400, versus only $11,097 for the all–U.S. portfolio. After 10 years, the lead of the globally diversified portfolio was greater: $32,975 versus $23,725. And after 20 years, at the end of 1989, there was no race any more. The global portfolio was worth $230,999, far ahead of the U.S. portfolio, $91,312.

As you can see in Table 9.2, return is only part of the story. The table shows that the global combination had less risk by *every measurement except the worst 36 months.*

In those 38 years, an initial investment of $100,000 in Portfolio 5 (see Figure 8.2 in the previous chapter) would have grown to about $6.5 million. That's without any international exposure. But when half the equity part of the portfolio was in international funds, the same initial investment grew to $9.5 million. This was a 46 percent increase in the ultimate return, and it came from changing only 30 percent of the makeup of the portfolio. Think about that the next time you read or hear that international funds aren't worth your time.

If you still aren't sure of the value of international funds, please join me in looking at the difference that they make to the typical retiree. We take up the topic of portfolio withdrawals in much more detail in Chapter 13. But this chapter would not be complete

**Table 9.1   Equity Investing with and without International Stocks, 1970–2007**

| Year | All U.S. Equities | 50/50 International Equities/U.S. Equities |
|------|-------------------|-------------------------------------------|
| 1970 | −2.4 | −4.1 |
| 1971 | 16.0 | 29.3 |
| 1972 | 9.8 | 27.6 |
| 1973 | −24.3 | −19.5 |
| 1974 | −23.0 | −24.5 |
| 1975 | 49.7 | 47.5 |
| 1976 | 42.2 | 23.4 |
| 1977 | 7.3 | 25.7 |
| 1978 | 13.9 | 31.7 |
| 1979 | 28.4 | 13.8 |
| 1980 | 27.1 | 26.9 |
| 1981 | 4.3 | 1.9 |
| 1982 | 25.6 | 12.0 |
| 1983 | 34.4 | 31.4 |
| 1984 | 1.7 | 4.6 |
| 1985 | 26.3 | 42.2 |
| 1986 | 11.5 | 33.5 |
| 1987 | −2.3 | 17.9 |
| 1988 | 22.7 | 26.7 |
| 1989 | 18.7 | 24.1 |
| 1990 | −18.3 | −14.5 |
| 1991 | 36.6 | 27.6 |
| 1992 | 18.8 | 2.8 |
| 1993 | 18.2 | 28.7 |
| 1994 | −0.7 | 3.0 |
| 1995 | 33.5 | 17.7 |
| 1996 | 19.7 | 11.8 |
| 1997 | 27.7 | 5.7 |
| 1998 | 4.6 | 5.7 |
| 1999 | 16.1 | 23.1 |
| 2000 | 2.1 | −5.2 |
| 2001 | 7.6 | −2.6 |
| 2002 | −15.7 | −10.5 |
| 2003 | 43.8 | 48.8 |
| 2004 | 17.0 | 22.2 |
| 2005 | 6.1 | 12.5 |
| 2006 | 17.3 | 22.3 |
| 2007 | −4.4 | 3.7 |

**Table 9.1  Equity Investing with and without
International Stocks, 1970–2007** *(Continued)*

|  | All U.S. Equities | 50/50 International Equities/U.S. Equities |
|---|---|---|
| Annual return | 12.1 | 13.7 |
| Standard deviation | 16.6 | 14.2 |
| Worst month | −25.3 | −18.8 |
| Worst 3 months | −30.9 | −22.1 |
| Worst 12 months | −34.6 | −35.4 |
| Worst 36 months | −36.0 | −23.6 |
| Worst 60 months | −29.0 | −10.0 |

**Assumptions**
1. Monthly rebalancing.
2. Management fee of 1% charged monthly.
3. U.S. allocation is 25% in each: LC, SC, LCV, SCV
4. International allocation is:
   January 1970 through December 1974: 50% LC, 50% SC
   January 1975 through December 1986: 25% LC, 25% LCV, 50% SC
   January 1987 through December 1994: 20% each in LC, LCV, EM; 40% in SC
   January 1995 through current: 20% each in LC, LCV, EM, SC, SCV

**Table 9.2  Results of Equity Investing with and without
International Stocks, 1970–2007**

|  | All U.S. Equities | 50/50 International Equities/U.S. Equities |
|---|---|---|
| Annualized return | 12.1 | 13.7 |
| $10,000 grew to | $774,684 | $1,335,529 |
| Standard deviation | 16.6 | 14.2 |
| Worst month | −25.3 | −18.8 |
| Worst 12 months | −30.9 | −22.1 |
| Worst 36 months | −34.6 | −35.4 |
| Worst 60 months | −36.0 | −23.6 |

without making the point that international funds can play a special role for retirees. The key concept for the moment is *volatility*.

When investors are accumulating assets, volatility may be uncomfortable, but it doesn't actually hurt unless it spooks those investors into abandoning a good strategy. But for investors who are regularly withdrawing money from their portfolios, volatility is a major threat.

Let me state four basic points before I back them up with a table of figures.

1. The biggest risk that retirees face is running out of money prematurely—in other words, before they run out of life.
2. A portfolio that's being asked to support regular withdrawals—especially withdrawals that increase over the years to keep up with inflation—has very different needs than a portfolio that's merely trying to accumulate assets.
3. Stability, or the lack of big losses, is critical to keep such a portfolio alive for many years. Even one terrible year can ruin things.
4. International stocks provide the stability that can help a lot to make that difference.

Table 9.3 shows the year-by-year results for three variations of a balanced portfolio, half of which remains in fixed-income funds. I believe this is a suitable allocation for retired people who want a reasonable combination of high returns (from equities) and low volatility (from fixed-income funds).

The table shows one portfolio with no international stocks, another with 15 percent in international stocks, and a third with 25 percent in international stocks. (That's equivalent to zero, 30 percent, and 50 percent of the equity part of the portfolio.) The figures in each column represent the value of the portfolio at the end of the year.

This table is oriented toward taking fixed annual withdrawals in retirement. We generated this table assuming you started with $1 million at the beginning of 1970 and took out $60,000 for living expenses at the start of the year. We further assumed that at the start of each subsequent year, you withdrew 3.5 percent more than you had in the previous year—thus, $62,100 for living expenses in 1971, $64,274 for 1972, and so forth. This corresponds to an assumed inflation rate of 3.5 percent per year.

The purpose of Table 9.3 is to show the value that international funds can make in a retirement portfolio.

The good news is that none of these three variations came even close to running out of money. The disturbing news is that in the early 1970s, the portfolio with no international equity funds lost 28 percent of its initial value (as it fell to $720,668). In my experience, most retirees would not be likely to stay the course after losing 28 percent of their money. And unfortunately, when people bail out, they often become easy prey for financial salespeople—sometimes with disastrous results.

The portfolio with 25 percent in international stocks, by contrast, had lost only about 21 percent of its initial value by the end of 1974 – still a significant loss but one that is more likely to be tolerable.

**Table 9.3    Retiring on $1 Million with and without International Equities**

| Withdrawal at Start of Year | Year | 0% International | 15% International | 25% International |
|---|---|---|---|---|
| $60,000 | 1970 | $994,663 | $986,472 | $980,512 |
| $62,100 | 1971 | $1,030,230 | $1,059,078 | $1,077,690 |
| $64,274 | 1972 | $1,032,683 | $1,111,320 | $1,165,545 |
| $66,523 | 1973 | $860,715 | $946,568 | $1,005,899 |
| $68,851 | 1974 | $720,668 | $792,336 | $840,905 |
| $71,261 | 1975 | $826,429 | $911,969 | $969,499 |
| $73,755 | 1976 | $940,309 | $1,002,003 | $1,039,147 |
| $76,337 | 1977 | $905,394 | $1,016,203 | $1,089,561 |
| $79,009 | 1978 | $892,284 | $1,054,628 | $1,167,303 |
| $81,774 | 1979 | $943,599 | $1,091,356 | $1,187,718 |
| $84,636 | 1980 | $1,000,666 | $1,169,345 | $1,278,770 |
| $87,598 | 1981 | $974,160 | $1,145,715 | $1,255,112 |
| $90,664 | 1982 | $1,104,762 | $1,274,158 | $1,373,218 |
| $93,837 | 1983 | $1,214,161 | $1,406,227 | $1,515,978 |
| $97,122 | 1984 | $1,202,174 | $1,420,184 | $1,546,841 |
| $100,521 | 1985 | $1,341,683 | $1,664,033 | $1,865,273 |
| $104,039 | 1986 | $1,390,140 | $1,848,550 | $2,161,181 |
| $107,681 | 1987 | $1,305,935 | $1,869,052 | $2,281,904 |
| $111,449 | 1988 | $1,362,704 | $2,025,034 | $2,515,807 |
| $115,350 | 1989 | $1,443,191 | $2,240,038 | $2,839,341 |
| $119,387 | 1990 | $1,253,725 | $2,036,327 | $2,632,502 |
| $123,566 | 1991 | $1,415,706 | $2,349,334 | $3,038,249 |
| $127,891 | 1992 | $1,453,359 | $2,401,026 | $3,053,248 |
| $132,367 | 1993 | $1,500,443 | $2,646,842 | $3,465,396 |
| $137,000 | 1994 | $1,335,017 | $2,486,652 | $3,321,072 |
| $141,795 | 1995 | $1,484,804 | $2,812,751 | $3,717,300 |
| $146,758 | 1996 | $1,486,059 | $2,902,197 | $3,830,806 |
| $151,894 | 1997 | $1,560,970 | $3,043,932 | $3,917,703 |
| $157,210 | 1998 | $1,502,695 | $3,100,988 | $4,044,020 |
| $162,713 | 1999 | $1,437,891 | $3,212,129 | $4,290,293 |
| $168,408 | 2000 | $1,357,640 | $3,187,035 | $4,248,636 |
| $174,302 | 2001 | $1,280,156 | $3,167,522 | $4,195,370 |
| $180,402 | 2002 | $1,079,576 | $2,988,794 | $4,059,911 |
| $186,717 | 2003 | $1,088,698 | $3,464,212 | $4,818,876 |
| $193,252 | 2004 | $985,039 | $3,660,339 | $5,219,089 |
| $200,015 | 2005 | $813,119 | $3,664,633 | $5,373,820 |
| $207,016 | 2006 | $662,381 | $3,851,542 | $5,802,226 |
| $214,262 | 2007 | $500,226 | $4,198,174 | $6,550,423 |

As you follow the numbers down the table, you can see that by the first few years of the 21st century, the all-U.S. portfolio was sputtering rapidly and inevitably toward going broke. The portfolios that included international funds were very robust and in no danger of running out of money.

## Emerging Markets Funds

The best way to diversify an equity portfolio is to include assets that have a good chance of providing premium returns at reasonable risk. Ideally, they should not be highly correlated with the overall market. At least in theory, emerging markets funds meet both those tests.

Emerging markets represent the great growth potential of young economies. Think of the difference between IBM and Microsoft in the late 1980s.

The majority of the world's people live and work in emerging-markets countries, places like Brazil, Chile, Poland, Hungary, China, and Russia. The average age of their populations is lower than those of most developed countries. As these younger populations mature, millions of their people will become new investors and begin thinking about their retirement. That will raise the demand for stocks, which should in turn raise stock prices. There is potential for a number of other areas of the world to experience the type of stock market boom that flourished in the United States during the 1990s.

Emerging markets funds can be quite profitable. From 1988 through 2007, an MSCI emerging markets index appreciated at an annual rate of 16.3 percent, compared with 11.8 percent for the S&P 500 Index. Vanguard's emerging markets index fund rose 61 percent in 1999 and 57 percent in 2003; in the years 2004 through 2007, its annual gains averaged more than 30 percent.

However, emerging markets can take investors on a wild ride that's not suited for timid souls. Vanguard's fund fell by 16.8 percent in 1997 and dropped another 18.1 percent in 1998; it fell by 27 percent in 2000. In addition, less stringent accounting standards, scarce information, and lax laws all combine to make emerging markets stocks riskier investments than those of developed countries.

There are two ways investors can tame the high volatility of emerging markets: first, by using no-load mutual funds that diversify widely instead of concentrating on a single region such as Russia or Latin America; and second, by limiting these funds to no more than 10 percent of the equity part of a portfolio.

Emerging markets may be the frosting—but they are not the cake.

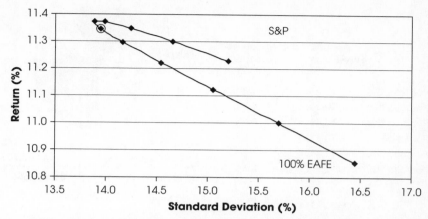

**Figure 9.1   The Balance of U.S. versus International Funds, 1970–2006**

If you're interested in living it up without outliving your money, this table should show you a very powerful way to do just that: Include international equities in your portfolio.

Let's move to Figure 9.1, comparing returns of U.S. versus international funds in the period 1970–2006*. You'll see right away that the S&P 500 Index had a higher return than the Morgan Stanley Europe Australia Far East Index (EAFE). But you'll see that a 50/50 combination of the two had a higher return than either index alone, while reducing the volatility of each of those components.

With that, we're ready to take the final step in putting together Your Ideal Portfolio. You see this in Figure 9.2, Portfolio 6. This step allocates half of the equities part of the portfolio to international funds and then splits that portion five ways.

This is a good place to sum up the past four chapters. We have outlined five relatively simple steps to improve the standard pension fund portfolio. First, we reconstituted the fixed-income part of the portfolio to include intermediate-term and short-term bonds as well as U.S. Treasury inflation-protected securities. Second, we added real estate investment trusts. Third, we included small-company funds. Fourth, we added value funds. And fifth, we added funds that invest in several important international equity asset classes.

---

* Figure 9.1 shows the curve of blending U.S. and international funds from 1970 only through 2006, not through 2007 as is the case with all the similar graphs in this book. I chose to use this time period in this case because the resulting curve is easy for the eye to quickly comprehend. For reasons that are mainly the quirk of statistics, the curve of returns from 1970 through 2007 appears to be almost a straight line which is not meaningful visually. You'll see that graph at the end of this chapter as Figure 9.3.

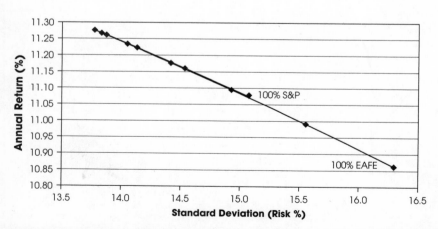

|  | Annualized Return | Annualized Standard Deviation |
|---|---|---|
| Portfolio One | 10.2% | 11.2% |
| Portfolio Two | 10.2% | 10.6% |
| Portfolio Three | 10.5% | 9.9% |
| Portfolio Four | 10.7% | 10.2% |
| Portfolio Five | 11.6% | 11.0% |
| Portfolio Six | 12.7% | 10.8% |

| | |
|---|---|
| Portfolio Six | $9,507,765 |
| Portfolio One | $4,066,109 |
| Difference | $5,441,656 |

**$100,000 grew to $9,507,656**

**Figure 9.2    Portfolio 6, January 1970 – December 2007**

Portfolio 6 is the result of those steps. Compared with Portfolio 1, our starting point, this combination subjects investors to less risk while it adds 2.5 percentage points of long-term annual return—an increase of 24 percent. And as you can see in Figure 9.2, the theoretical payoff for a $100,000 investment more than doubled, from $4.1 million to $9.5 million.

At this point, you know how to build a portfolio that will harness a world of investment opportunities to help you reach your goals.

**Figure 9.3    The balance of U.S. versus International Funds, 1970–2007**

# Controlling Risks

*Trust in Allah, but tie your camel.*

—Arab proverb

A recurring theme throughout this book is risk, and finally the topic gets its own chapter. I haven't consolidated every part of the risk discussion into one place because it is a topic that needs to be brought up again and again. I hope you'll get used to thinking of it as an integral part of investing. In this chapter we move from risk as an abstract concept to risk as a cold, hard reality with specific numbers. There's no perfect way to know in advance precisely what level of loss you can tolerate, but there are numerous ways to help you get a handle on it.

One of the most important things we do in our company is interview investors about their risk tolerance. We use a series of questions to help us to get an authentic look at how each person deals with adversity. In some cases we ask the same question more than once, just in different ways.

Ultimately, it's necessary to get specific about making the trade-offs between risk and expected return. In workshops and with clients, we use a table of numbers to show the results (in the past, because that's all we have) of various combinations of equity funds and fixed-income funds, each with its own set of returns and risks.

With this table, an investor who has carefully thought about his needs and risk tolerance can choose a combination of investments that's likely to provide the right combination of growth and comfort.

In many years of counseling individual investors, I've seen again and again how tough it is for people to know in advance how much risk they can actually stomach. Your risk tolerance has a large emotional (and therefore somewhat unpredictable) component.

In the abstract, risk is elusive. When you're basking in the warmth of summer, it's hard to be too serious about the warm clothes you'll need in winter. And when you're dreaming of a pleasant and prosperous retirement, it's easy to gloss over the fact that you could lose half—or more—of your money if you make the wrong investments.

In practice, your risk tolerance is probably more complex than a single number. Most people have to make monthly mortgage payments. I don't think they have much tolerance for risking the money earmarked for that next mortgage payment. By contrast, if you're saving for a goal 10 to 20 years in the future, the prospect of an interim loss should be less worrisome.

In my own case, I have three portfolios, each with its own risk tolerance. I have a very conservatively invested portfolio of money set aside for my retirement. Although I have no plans to stop working anytime soon, when the time finally comes for me to retire, I want to be sure that money is there to take care of me and my family. My risk tolerance for this money is very low.

My second portfolio is money I don't expect to ever need. I intend that it will someday go to my children, and it's invested aggressively to seek a high return, based on what I consider their risk tolerance, not mine.

My third portfolio is probably off the charts in terms of risk. Some people would consider this to be play money. While I never buy individual stocks, from time to time I invest for fun in the ventures of friends and people I know. I don't expect a high return from these investments. Twice I have helped friends get started in the financial services business. And once I invested in a movie in which my son was involved.

I'm not suggesting that you adopt my plan. But I hope you'll realize that you might have more than just one pot of money and more than only one level of tolerance for risk. For example, I think some retirees shortchange their children by being much too conservative with money that they (the parents) will never need.

In my workshop I ask how many participants are willing to lose half or more of their money. I don't see many hands raised—perhaps one out of every hundred people. Then I ask how many people have the majority of their money invested in individual stocks. Lots of hands go up. This tells me that many of the people who come to my workshops simply don't understand how much risk they have been taking.

My company has developed an excellent series of questions that can help you figure out your own tolerance for risk. There are no right or wrong answers. The best answers are the most honest answers. Here are 11 questions for you to think about, each one related to risk, along with my thoughts on what your answers might indicate:

1. For a potential annual return of 8 to 10 percent, you would tolerate a maximum one-year loss of _____ percent.
2. For a potential annual return of 10 to 12 percent, you would tolerate a maximum one-year loss of _____ percent.
3. For a potential annual return of 12 to 15 percent, you would tolerate a maximum one-year loss of _____ percent.

     *Comment:* In my experience, most retirees can meet their needs with returns of 8 to 10 percent at very reasonable levels of risk. It's rare that any investor truly needs more than 10 to 12 percent, and we usually don't even need to ask the third question. But we ask that third question in order to see if people understand that higher returns go hand in hand with higher levels of risk. Anybody who wants a return of 10 to 12 percent and can't tolerate an interim loss of more than 10 percent is heading for big trouble. If you need a 10 percent return, you should be prepared for a one-year loss of at least 15 percent. In seeking a return of 12 to 15 percent, you'd better be ready to lose 20 to 50 percent at some point along the way.

4. What past investments have you made that pleased you? Why did they please you?

     *Comment:* It won't surprise you to know that investors always answer this question by naming something that made money for them. And that is invariably something that's part of an asset class that was profitable at that time. Rarely do people say they were pleased with an investment because it had low risk.

5. What past investments did not please you? Why were you displeased? Would you make a similar investment again? How did you respond to your displeasure with this investment?

*Comment:* The investments listed in answer to this question are invariably ones that either lost money or made much less than they should have in the view of the investor. The "why" question is a way to get investors to think about their own relationship with taking risks.

The third part of this question is particularly interesting. If you are willing to do something worthwhile (and for investors, taking risks is not only worthwhile but necessary) a second time, even after being burned the first time, you may truly understand the concept of risk.

Sometimes the same investment, for example an S&P 500 Index fund, is listed as the answer to both question 3 and question 4, the only difference being the timing of the investment. (The Vanguard 500 Index Fund severely disappointed many investors with a 22.2 percent loss in 2002; but it must have thoroughly delighted many investors with its 28.5 percent gain in 2003.)

The final part of this question is the all-important one. The most accurate indicator of your actual risk tolerance is probably what you will do in the face of adversity. And I believe that your past actions strongly indicate your likely future actions.

If you made and followed a thoughtful plan for dealing with losses, that suggests you have a healthy understanding of risk and can deal with it well. But if you looked at the newspapers one day and sold in panic after suddenly realizing you had lost money, that suggests you should not be exposed to high levels of risk.

6. On a scale of 1 to 10, with 1 being extremely conservative and 10 extremely aggressive, how would you characterize yourself as an investor?

*Comment:* People who rate themselves 7 and above usually believe they are able to accept quite a bit of risk. However, we often find that the answer to this question is inconsistent with other answers. This indicates that more discussion is warranted.

This is a good example of something else that's useful about this quiz. Many times we'll find that the questions are answered differently by a husband and wife. When the differences are significant, this gives us a chance to start a conversation that can help a couple see that their risk tolerance may not be as straightforward as they (or as one of them) previously thought.

7. Choose the statement that best describes your overall investment objectives:
   • Growing assets without concern for current income.
   • Growing assets somewhat, while generating current income.
   • Generating current income and preserving capital.

   *Comment:* This question is carefully worded to force an investor to make a choice rather than indicate a desire for every possible result. It's also helpful to us so we can judge whether the answer to this question is consistent with other answers.

8. If you invested $100,000 seeking a long-term return of 10 to 12 percent, choose the maximum short-term (one-year) loss you would accept:
   • More than $15,000.
   • $10,000 to $15,000.
   • Less than $10,000.

   *Comment:* This is essentially the same as the first question on our list. We include it in order to see if the answer matches the earlier answer. What we're looking for is consistency (or the lack of it). Sometimes people believe they are willing to tolerate percentage losses that they won't accept when those losses are stated in real dollars.

   We once had a client who was certain he could tolerate a loss of 10 percent of his portfolio. But panic unexpectedly struck him after a loss of only 4 percent. The reason: That 4 percent was equal to the number of dollars he was once accustomed to earning in a full year. That thought was simply too tough for him emotionally.

9. Indicate when you expect to need (or plan to use) the money you are investing or have invested:
   • 10 or more years.
   • 6 to 10 years.
   • Less than 6 years.

*Comment:* This gives us some essential information. Money that will be needed in only a few years should not be exposed to large potential losses. Conversely, an investor who won't need money for decades should not be obsessively concerned with short-term comfort.

10. Pick one of the following statements
    - I am willing to tolerate substantial swings in my portfolio value to maximize growth.
    - I am willing to tolerate small swings in my portfolio value, though this might mean lower growth.
    - I am willing to tolerate only slight deviations in my portfolio value despite slower overall growth.

    *Comment:* This is merely one more way to ask the question that we've been posing again and again. An investor at peace with the trade-off between risk and return will answer most of these questions in a consistent manner. More often, we see somewhat different answers when we pose the question in different ways.

11. Pick one of the following:
    - After investing, I generally know that ups and downs are inevitable and check the results infrequently.
    - After investing, I generally pay attention but recognize that values change constantly and do not worry excessively.
    - After investing, I generally watch the markets daily and calculate my gains or losses frequently.

    *Comment:* The third choice is a red flag for us. An investor who tallies up gains and losses every day may be simply a meticulous bookkeeper. But he or she might be extremely nervous. Whatever it is, we want to understand the reason.

No single question does the whole job. But when all these questions are honestly and thoughtfully answered and discussed, they provide an excellent window into an investor's ability to deal with risk. Unfortunately, most financial advisers don't take the time to go over these topics very thoroughly with their clients. I wish more of them did. If you have thoughtfully completed these steps, you're ready to get down to numbers.

We've already thoroughly covered equity diversification as a way to reduce risk. Beyond that, the most important thing you can do to control the level of risk you take is to adjust the mix of fixed-income and equity investments in your portfolio. This adjustment is one of the most fundamental decisions faced by every investor. Some investors prefer a total equity portfolio for its superior growth prospects. Others invest exclusively in fixed-income funds, wanting to completely avoid the risks of the stock market.

For most people, comfort and need intersect somewhere between those two extremes. How far should you go in one direction or the other? One excellent place to start your search is with a 50/50 mix of equity funds and fixed-income funds. It's easy to understand and to keep balanced. And I have found that it works very well for people who are retired or nearing retirement.

## Balancing Risk and Return, 1970–2007

A 50/50 split isn't for everybody, of course. Fortunately there is a wide range of possibilities. You'll see examples of this in Table 10.1, which contains some important numbers for investors. The numbers are excerpted from a more complete table that's available at FundAdvice.com as part of an article called "Fine-Tuning Your Asset Allocation." This full table includes year-by-year results of these combinations as well as additional risk measurements for each.

Each line in the table represents a mix of global equities (along the lines described in Chapters 6 through 9) and fixed-income investments

**Table 10.1   Balancing Risk and Return, 1970–2007**

| Global Equity Percent | Fixed-Income Percent | Annualized Return | Standard Deviation | Worst 12 Months | Worst 60 Months |
|---|---|---|---|---|---|
| 0 | 100 | 7.0 | 5.6 | −4.8 | 14.1 |
| 10 | 90 | 7.8 | 5.3 | −4.0 | 25.8 |
| 20 | 80 | 8.5 | 5.6 | −5.9 | 27.2 |
| 30 | 70 | 9.2 | 6.4 | −10.0 | 25.9 |
| 40 | 60 | 9.9 | 7.5 | −14.0 | 21.2 |
| 50 | 50 | 10.6 | 8.9 | −17.8 | 16.4 |
| 60 | 40 | 11.3 | 10.4 | −21.5 | 11.7 |
| 70 | 30 | 11.9 | 12.0 | −25.1 | 7.0 |
| 80 | 20 | 12.6 | 13.7 | −28.5 | 2.3 |
| 90 | 10 | 13.2 | 15.5 | −31.9 | −2.3 |
| 100 | 0 | 13.7 | 17.3 | −35.1 | −6.9 |

(as described at the end of Chapter 6). As you go down the page, each successive line includes an additional 10 percent incremental exposure to equities.

As you will see (and as you would probably expect), adding equities brings an increase in return and an increase in risk, represented here by standard deviation and worst 12-month and 60-month periods. The figures represent results from the years 1970 through 2007. (Worst periods are rolling measurements that don't necessarily correspond with calendar years. Each can start at the beginning of any calendar month. Thus April 1, 1998, through March 31, 1999, is one 12-month period.)

Notice that the 50/50 mix I recommend as a starting point achieved a compound annual return of 10.6 percent. That is more than three-quarters of the return of the 100 percent equity combination. The statistical risk of the 50/50 portfolio, a standard deviation of 8.9 percent, was just over half that of the all-equity model. In other words, the 50/50 combination gave investors most of the gain with only about half the pain. The 60/40 mix (which we saw in Chapter 6 as the standard pension plan model) reduced the volatility of the all-equity portfolio by about 40 percent while capturing more than 80 percent of the return.

In this 38-year period an all-equity portfolio invested exclusively in the S&P 500 Index would have returned 11.2 percent. That is nearly the same as the 60/40 global portfolio.

Thus we see two ways investors could have earned about the same returns. But of course those investors couldn't know that in advance, so risk becomes very important. Measured by its standard deviation of 16.6 percent, the S&P 500 Index was much more risky than the globally diversified 60/40 combination.

The worst 60-month period ended with a cumulative loss of 17.5 percent for the index, compared with a gain of 11.7 percent for the 60/40 combination.

Getting approximately the same return at greatly reduced risk might strike you as merely a nice idea. But I assure you, it's one of the most important concerns for retired people—and relatively few retirees understand it as well as they should.

In my workshops, I present a large table based on a $1 million portfolio starting in 1970 with withdrawals of $60,000, increasing at the rate of 3.5 percent per year. (If this is starting to sound familiar, then you've been paying attention.) This table shows year-by-year results for 12 portfolios, ranging from all fixed-income to 100 percent global equity, plus one that contains only the Standard & Poor's 500 Index.

I particularly like to compare the columns for the S&P 500 Index and the 50/50 combination, since they have produced nearly identical long-term returns. What's different about them is volatility, or risk. The S&P 500 Index is much more volatile, and in a retirement portfolio that is sometimes literally the kiss of death.

By January 2005, the Standard & Poor's 500 Index portfolio was broke. The 50/50 portfolio ended 2004 worth more than $6.3 million. That difference is the price of volatility.

The best way to use Table 10.1 is to start by writing down two numbers: the target return you need and your largest acceptable one-year loss in percentage terms. Start with the return figure and scan the table to find the line that would give you what you need. Check to see how the one-year loss stacks up against your wish. Assuming that is not a perfect match, find the line that matches your self-determined risk tolerance and you'll see the return you would have received. Can you find a way to achieve your goals with that return? If so, you've got a pretty good idea of the allocation that's likely to work for you.

But what if you need the returns from an allocation that has too much risk? Your first impulse may be to go for the desired return and figure you'll tough it out through the bad times. That's usually a big mistake. If your needs straddle two columns, you should choose the one that has the right level of risk.

There are three reasons for that. First, remember that the figures in this table are not predictions of the future, only results from the past. And the past is a more reliable indicator of risk than of returns. For any given combination of assets, the pattern of volatility will be more constant and more predictable than the pattern of return.

Second, risk matters much more than most people think.

Finally, it is never acceptable or advisable to manage a portfolio in violation of your risk tolerance. Year after year, decade after decade, I have seen investors get in trouble by taking more risk than they should. They're the ones who suffer serious losses and bail out when prices are down—just the opposite of what they should be doing if they were buying low and selling high.

If you learn only one lesson from this book, I hope it's this one: Never ignore your emotions or your better judgment in order to chase higher returns. If you prudently choose to take lower risks and wind up with a lower return, you might have to work longer before you can retire. You might have to spend less (and save more) before retiring. You might have to spend less after you retire.

But you'll preserve your peace of mind. And in the end, peace of mind is priceless. You now have the tools at your disposal to get it from your investments.

# CHAPTER

# 11

# Meet Your Enemies

## EXPENSES AND TAXES

*Beware of expenses: A small leak will sink a great ship.*
—Benjamin Franklin

Investors should never forget that quotation from Ben Franklin. You can do everything else right, but if you let your investment gains leak out of your portfolio, your money won't be there when you need it.

Expenses and taxes are like leaks. Even small ones can cripple the best-laid plans. Over a 20-year period, paying an extra 1 percent in annual expenses can reduce your ending account balance by 17 percent. Stated another way, this means that the more you pay for investment services, the less chance you'll have enough money to retire.

If your goal is to accumulate $1 million in 25 years and you can save $1,000 a month, you'll need a return (after expenses) of 8.3 percent. But if you pay out even one-half of one percentage point in unnecessary expenses every year, earning only 7.8 percent, you will end up nearly $80,000 short, with only $920,688.

One half a percentage point of return may seem insignificant. But in this example, that extra half a percentage point will have cost you the equivalent of more than six and a half years of the $1,000 payments you made into your account over a quarter of a century.

Unfortunately, this sort of waste happens much too often for my taste. Morningstar Inc. reports the expense ratios for thousands of mutual funds, individually and by categories. In Morningstar's nine broad style-box categories for U.S. equity funds, such as large-cap growth, mid-cap blend, and small-cap value, average annual expense ratios in late 2007 ranged from a low of 1.27 percent (large blend) to a high of 1.61 percent (small growth). The average of all those nine category averages was 1.41 percent. Those numbers represent fees charged directly to investors by mutual funds.

When those funds are held in non–retirement (taxable) accounts, Uncle Sam takes a cut almost every year, too. Morningstar computes an average annual tax cost for each mutual fund it tracks. (This is the tax cost of owning the fund and assumes that you don't sell any shares.)

The average annual tax cost of the 12 largest diversified U.S. equity funds over the 10 years ending October 31, 2007, was 1.07 percent. The average expense ratio of these 12 funds was 0.49 percent, for a combined leak, on average, of 1.56 percentage points per year. And that is for a group of funds with well-below-average expenses.

Those expense ratios don't include the cost of heavy portfolio turnover. Many investors in the late 1990s were enamored of technology funds, which have portfolio turnover averaging 178 percent per year—more than eight times the turnover of the equity index funds we recommend. That heavy trading drives costs up (and thus drives returns down). Obviously, investment managers and salespeople deserve to be paid, and investors should expect to pay for legitimate expenses. Taxes also must be paid. But if you overpay, you erode your returns and give back money that rightly should belong to you.

Investors leave money on the table in many ways. They invest in tax-inefficient funds. They trade too often. They fail to take full advantage of tax-sheltered accounts such as IRAs and 401(k)s. (The AARP reported in 2007 that only

7 percent of workers are contributing to IRAs, a figure that's consistent with reports from the Internal Revenue Service.)

Investors overpay their taxes because they keep poor records and thus pay taxes twice on the same income when they finally sell. The same thing happens when they invest in mutual funds immediately before taxable distributions, thus being taxed on part of their own investments. On the expense side, investors who don't know or don't care pay more than they need to for sales commissions, recurring expenses, and trading costs.

Many investors constantly seek higher returns, which are often available to those who take higher risks. But there's a risk-free way to achieve higher returns, and that's to limit the erosion of taxes and expenses. This chapter shows how to do that.

This is a chapter the investment industry hopes you'll skip over quickly.

Many things are beyond investors' control. But expenses and taxes are two very important exceptions. If you pay careful attention to this topic, you will benefit. If you neglect it, you will pay for your negligence. It's as simple as that.

Let's tackle expenses first, then taxes. There are three major areas of expenses that investors pay: sales expenses, operating expenses, and trading costs.

To the greatest extent possible, Wall Street likes to mask expenses and redirect investors' attention elsewhere. To manage your expenses effectively, you'll have to first be able to recognize them, then make the choice, when you have it, to accept them, limit them, or eliminate them.

Trading costs are just that: the expense any investor incurs when buying and selling stocks, bonds, and other securities. In mutual funds, trading costs are usually neither explicitly disclosed nor subject to much control by fund shareholders. The best way to keep these costs under control is to buy low-turnover mutual funds such as index funds.

At or near the opposite end of the scale are technology funds, which as a group have average annual portfolio turnover of 178 percent. Aside from the costs of all that trading, think for a second what that figure means to investors. If you buy a technology fund, you might think you are hiring a manager to make smart long-term choices of the most promising companies and technological advances. But 178 percent annual turnover suggests that these managers are mostly engaged in frantically chasing short-term moves.

Investors can do much more about recurring expenses and selling expenses—but only if they take a proactive role.

Mutual fund investors pay management expenses that include all the normal costs to run a fund and support existing shareholders: accountants, custodians, lawyers, transfer agents, an annual meeting, administration, salaries, rent, printing, statements, taxes, regulatory compliance, and so forth.

These recurring expenses are relatively easy to identify. Every mutual fund must report what it charges investors on an annual basis. For example, the giant Fidelity Contrafund's expense ratio is 0.89 percent per year. This is a comparatively large leak.

Consider that frugal investors who choose index funds can get access to the same asset class (U.S. large-cap growth stocks) for 0.22 percent at Vanguard.

Sometimes Contrafund outperforms the indexes, but that extra performance is not reliable. However, the higher expenses that fund charges are quite reliable. My advice: When you can, stack the odds in your favor by using low-cost index funds.

You may think money market funds are generic products, easily interchangeable. But they aren't. Most taxable money funds invest similarly, and the raw returns of their portfolios—in other words, what the funds receive before they charge any expenses to shareholders—are very similar if not (as some studies have shown) essentially identical. But expenses charged to shareholders can make a huge difference in money funds. Investors who ignore this detail can pay dearly for their lack of attention.

Here's an example we found early in 2008. Vanguard Prime Money Market Fund (VMMXX) had an expense ratio of 0.24 percent and a seven-day yield (this is after all expenses have been charged to shareholders) of 3.64 percent. On the same day, we checked the Alliance Bernstein Exchange Reserves Fund (AEBXX). The Alliance Bernstein web site says this fund's objective is "to provide maximum current income consistent with safety of principal and liquidity."

However, Alliance Bernstein's idea of the meaning of "maximum current income" is certainly different from mine. The fund's class B shares levy expenses of 1.61 percent, more than six times those of the Vanguard fund. The seven-day yield of the Alliance Bernstein Exchange Reserves fund was only 2.43 percent. I hesitate to accuse this fund family of greed, but I cannot think of any sensible justification for charging such high expenses in a money market fund that's trying to maximize current income for its shareholders.

On the surface, these two funds might look the same. But investors who chose the Alliance Bernstein entry gave up one-third of the current yield they could have had at Vanguard—probably without realizing it. This is a leak.

Mutual funds aren't alone in charging recurring fees. At many brokerage firms, investors with accounts smaller than $50,000 are charged maintenance fees of $100 or more a year. I'm not saying this is a rip-off, because it costs money to keep an account open. But it certainly is a leak.

Investors usually have a choice about the brokerage house they deal with. But that's not the case with employees who are charged up to 2 percent per year for the costs of administering their companies' 401(k) plans—in addition, of course, to regular mutual fund fees. This is a leak.

Most mutual fund companies and other financial institutions charge annual maintenance fees of $10 or more for IRA accounts. That fee is often waived for larger accounts, but investors who don't consolidate their IRAs can easily pay $100 a year this way. This is a leak.

Variable annuities are notorious, often charging expenses that total more than 2.5 percentage points. In addition, investors in annuities often must pay an annual contract fee of $30 to $50. In 2007 Morningstar said variable annuity expenses averaged 2.4 percent and annual fees averaged $37. In addition, some annuity contracts charge a fee every time an investor swaps between investments within the plan. (About half of all investors in annuities wind up paying surrender charges for cashing out before a minimum contract period that can be 10 years or more.) These are leaks.

Each of these leaks may seem small by itself. Wall Street likes it that way. After all, how much time and energy will somebody spend to avoid a $10 annual IRA fee? Expenses are usually disclosed in writing, but they are rarely emphasized, and investors often receive the disclosure only after they have committed their money.

The cure? Remember that investment firms are not charities. Always ask about expenses. If you don't see an expense disclosure, ask somebody to point it out to you. Always seek less expensive ways to achieve what you need. When you hear a pitch about some great product or program, you should be at least as interested in how much it costs as you are in how much a salesperson thinks it will return.

Sales costs also are largely within investors' control. These include brokerage commissions, sales loads on mutual fund purchases, and extraordinary expense ratios charged to owners of some classes of fund shares. (I could easily write a book on this topic alone, but for now, part of a chapter will have to do.)

Mutual funds essentially come in two flavors: load funds and no-load funds. In this context, when you see the word *load*, think *sales commission.*

When you invest $10,000 in a no-load fund, the entire $10,000 is invested on your behalf and goes to work for you. Because there's no sales commission, you won't find out about these funds from brokers or financial advisers who are compensated only by sales commissions. You must find these funds yourself (or pay an adviser to find them for you) and make your own decisions about them. Doing it yourself—with the help you'll find in this book—could potentially add hundreds or even thousands of dollars to your nest egg.

In a load fund, a sales commission is immediately subtracted from your investment. This is the equivalent of experiencing a huge drop in the stock market on your first day. Invest $10,000 in a fund with a 5.75 percent front-end load (a common arrangement for class A shares), and only $9,425 is invested for you. That's what your account will be worth at the end of the first day you own the fund.

The debate over the merits of load funds and no-load funds can be fierce. I'm going to give you my point of view, and I'll back up every bit of it. You'll find other points of view strongly held by people who sell funds, and by some of their customers. In the end, you'll have to make up your own mind.

I can't see any reason most well-informed investors should pay a sales commission to buy a fund. Certainly anybody who is capable of understanding this book can recognize and find good funds without paying for that service from a broker whose interests are almost certainly in conflict with those of the investor.

Some years back I wrote an article called "Ten Reasons Why You Should Never Buy a Load Fund." I'd like to discuss some of those points here.

I don't know how to say it any more bluntly than this: Sales loads don't do you any good. (In fact, they do the opposite, as we shall see.)

A mutual fund is really just a pool of money being managed to accomplish some purpose. The *load* is money paid to the salesperson who brings in the money. The commission doesn't help compensate the portfolio manager. It simply diverts money away from that manager by reducing the potential assets under management. (Your full $10,000 could be in the fund instead of only $9,425.) This is a leak.

Every study I've ever seen concludes that over long periods of time there is no statistically significant difference in the returns of all-load funds versus all no-load funds—assuming that you ignore the loads. But ignoring sales commissions is silly and misleading. Paying a load puts investors at an immediate disadvantage, because their portfolios never get the benefit of all the dollars that leave their pockets. Worse, that disadvantage grows over time.

The mathematics are simple, and you can figure them out yourself with a calculator. Imagine two funds with identical portfolio performance. One charges you a 5.75 percent front-end load, the other is no-load. Result: You will always have 6.1 percent more money in the no-load account than in the load account. (That figure represents the sales load when it is properly computed as a percentage of the amount actually invested. On a $10,000 investment, the $575 load is 6.1 percent of the $9,425 that is invested in the fund.) With a $10,000 investment in two funds that earn 10 percent annually, the difference after 15 years is $2,401. The load fund account has an ending balance of $39,371, versus $41,772 in the no-load fund.

Not all load funds have up-front sales commissions. Class B shares of load funds (sometimes incorrectly and misleadingly described by salespeople as "no-load") charge pointedly higher expense ratios instead of up-front sales loads. This robs performance as well.

Typically, class B shares charge a declining back-end load to investors who fail to leave their money in long enough for the extra expenses to cover the sales commission that wasn't collected up front. After a stipulated period, often seven years, class B shares convert to class A, and from that point their expense ratios decline, improving their performance.

For an example, consider the venerable Columbia Acorn Fund (ACRNX). Its no-load shares have an expense ratio of 0.74 percent. Its class A shares charge 1.02 percent and its class B shares charge

1.66 percent. All three share classes have the same underlying portfolio.

To see what these numbers mean in real life, consider an investor who makes a one-time $10,000 purchase in this fund. Let's assume that the underlying portfolio earns 10 percent per year, after the 0.74 percent expenses of the no-load shares. After 15 years, an investor in the no-load shares would have an account worth $41,772. An investor in the class B shares, on the other hand, would get a lower return for the first seven years, 9.08 percent to be exact, reflecting the higher expense ratio. Starting in the eighth year, after the original shares converted to class A shares, the expense ratio would decline and annual performance would increase to 9.72 percent.

After 15 years, the investor in class B shares would have an account worth $38,592. That's $3,180 less than in the no-load fund with exactly the same portfolio and the same manager. That difference is more than 30 percent of the investor's initial $10,000 investment, and it's entirely the result of higher sales and marketing charges that are taken out a little bit at a time for as long as the investor owns those class B shares.

Tens of thousands of investors pay these sales loads, whether they are hidden or disclosed, every year. The interesting question is whether they receive anything in return. Presumably such fees buy the advantage of having a salesperson choose funds.

But I don't believe that happens. I've seen thousands of investors' portfolios over the years, and I've found that most investors in load funds have poor asset allocation. Instead of balanced portfolios that would make their money work hard for them while keeping risks under control, most load-fund investors wind up with collections of funds that are easy to sell—primarily large-cap U.S. stock funds.

For long-term investors, loads are much higher than they seem. If you could avoid paying a $1,000 sales charge by investing in a no-load fund, and assuming the fund you bought and the fund you didn't buy each compounded at 10 percent, in 25 years you would wind up with nearly $11,000 more. In effect, the $1,000 load cost you $11,000. This is not a small leak. It's a huge leak.

Even when you pay a sales commission, you might not get what you think you are buying. Some fund salespeople say they earn their commissions by finding funds with the best managers. But what happens if, shortly after you buy into such a fund, the manager leaves to run some other fund? At best, you have paid for the track record of a manager who's not working for you. At worst, if you decide to follow that manager to a new load fund, you might wind up paying a second sales commission. Next time you're considering investing in any fund because of its manager, remember this: The best managers are the ones most likely to get new job offers.

Many investors in actively managed mutual funds, no doubt encouraged by advisers who earn commissions by selling them, apparently believe that all my hand-wringing about expenses is irrelevant when a particular fund achieves a superior return. On the surface, it would seem that investors need not care about expenses as long as a fund's return is satisfactory. That's because the fund's expense ratio is already taken into account when the return is calculated.

If a high expense ratio normally brought a premium return that investors could count on, then paying those higher expenses would be a rational choice. (Millions of investors must wish that smart investing were that simple!) However, every rigorous study that I'm familiar with on mutual fund performance shows exactly the opposite: Paying above-average expenses makes above-average performance *less* likely, not more likely. The reason is simple: Expenses don't enhance performance, they decrease performance. Every dollar you unnecessarily pay or lose now costs you not only that dollar but also the future earnings on that dollar.

I don't make many guarantees in this book. But I can guarantee you that the companies and people who provide financial services have all thought very carefully about how much to charge for those services. Investors who are casual about this subject are only hurting themselves.

Now let's tackle taxes. Entire libraries could be filled with tax information relevant to investors, but in real life, few people have the time or interest to pursue this topic at length. I'll take a moment to highlight some topics that relate to mutual fund investors. Please note that some of these points do not apply within tax-sheltered accounts such as IRAs and 401(k) plans.

Mutual funds with high portfolio turnover generate higher tax burdens than funds with lower turnover. The introduction to this chapter mentioned the annual tax cost (1.07 percentage points) of the 12 largest U.S. equity funds.

Even though most investors have their income and capital gains distributions reinvested, taxes must be paid on those distributions. Some fund managers care more about those taxes than others.

Setting aside continuing expenses, consider two of the largest U.S. equity funds, Vanguard 500 Index (VFINX) and Fidelity Magellan (FMAGX). For the 10 years ended October 31, 2007, Morningstar calculated the annual tax loss of these two funds: 0.44 percent for Vanguard, 1.18 percent for Magellan. This figure represents the percentage of their holdings that each fund's shareholders who were in the highest tax brackets would have paid in taxes year by year as a result of income and capital gains distributions. Think of the tax loss figure as a leak, a drag on performance.

For investors in taxable accounts, the combined annual expense and tax loss ratios add up to 1.71 percent for Magellan and 0.62 percent for Vanguard 500 Index. (By the way, Magellan's annual portfolio turnover was 41 percent, eight times that of Vanguard 500 Index. This burdens Magellan investors with more costs.) Which of these two funds would you rather own? Investors who take the trouble to find such information wind up with much more efficient portfolios. Those who don't bother wind up with big leaks.

Casual or sloppy fund investors sometimes pay taxes twice on the same income. Remember those capital gains and income distributions? I hope so, because you probably reinvested them in more fund shares. As a result, those distributions have become part of the tax basis of your investment in the fund. If you fail to increase your basis accordingly, you could report (and pay taxes on) larger gains than you actually have.

The solution is to keep good records so you know how much you paid for the shares you own. At the end of each calendar year, keep your annual fund statements (you can discard the interim statements). Most mutual funds now provide average cost information when you sell. But have your own records as a backup. Investors who sell zero-coupon bonds should also make sure they aren't reporting gains on which they have already paid taxes. This is a good example of why you might benefit from a professional tax adviser.

Investors pay too much in taxes when they neglect to use IRAs and other retirement accounts for which they are eligible. The Roth IRA and its younger cousin the Roth 401(k) are the most tax-efficient vehicles around; if you ignore them, you are essentially shooting yourself in the foot. Outside of these tax shelters, many investors ignore the opportunity to invest in tax-managed funds that are run specifically to keep the government's hands out of investors' pockets. We discuss those in the next chapter.

Another way that many investors pay unnecessary taxes is by incorrectly allocating assets between their taxable and tax-sheltered accounts. The general rule is that as much as possible, tax-efficient assets should go in taxable accounts while tax-inefficient assets belong in tax-sheltered accounts.

Here's what that means: Index equity funds and tax-managed funds belong in taxable (nonsheltered) accounts. Taxable fixed-income funds, real estate funds, and (for investors who own them against my recommendations) actively managed funds all belong in tax-sheltered accounts.

You may not be able to segregate all your assets that way. But to the extent you can, that's the division you should make.

## If You Already Own a Load Fund

If you already own one or more load funds, you won't necessarily benefit from selling them. What you should do depends partly on what class of shares you have and how long you have owned them.

If you bought class A shares, the kind with the load charged up front, the money you paid in a sales charge is simply gone. For practical purposes, you now own a no-load fund—unless you are charged a load for adding new money.

Once you buy class B shares, you are going to pay the full sales commission one way or another. There's no way to get out of it. If you hold the shares a given number of years (often six or seven), you'll pay the load in the form of extraordinarily high expenses for that time, and then the shares will automatically convert to class A shares, which have a lower expense ratio (and correspondingly higher performance). If you sell before the conversion date, you'll pay an exit fee, a back-end load that will effectively finish compensating the fund for the sales commission it paid.

If you own class B shares and you're thinking of selling them, it might make sense to wait until you pass an anniversary date that reduces the exit fee, which typically drops by one percentage point per year that you own the shares. But if that anniversary date is more than half a year away, the wait might not be worthwhile.

If you own class C shares, you'll pay the load in the form of extraordinary expenses for as long as you own the shares. These shares never convert to class A, so the expense ratio never drops. However, there's usually no exit fee after you have owned these shares for at least a year. In general, the sooner you sell class C shares, the better off you will be.

*(Continued)*

Whatever class of shares you own, it's not necessarily a good idea to hang on to a load fund. Even if, in the case of class B shares, you own the shares long enough to avoid a withdrawal fee, you may still be in a fund that isn't right for you because of the asset class of its portfolio.

Here's the best advice I can give you: Start with the asset allocation process described in this book and determine the best mix of asset classes for you. Then ask yourself: Does this load fund I own fit neatly in the plan that I should have? Does it have a good record, low expenses, low portfolio turnover, and reputable management? If all the answers are positive, keep the fund.

If you don't have a clear idea why you invested in the fund, or if it doesn't fit into the plan you have made for attaining your objectives, and if it's definitely something you would not invest in again, consider selling in order to find something that will be more suitable for you.

A final consideration concerns taxes. If a sale would result in a taxable capital gain, you'll have to weigh that cost against the cost of continuing to own a fund that you have determined is wrong for you. If the solution to this trade-off isn't obvious, enlist the help of a professional adviser who doesn't sell products (see Chapter 14).

Selling a load fund (or any other investment that you have determined may have been a mistake) probably won't be at the top of any list of things you want to do. It's the sort of move that's easy to put off. But putting it off might cost you thousands of dollars. If you do it as soon as you recognize it as a good idea, that move could ultimately be worth thousands of extra dollars.

I'd like to mention one more tax mistake that mutual fund investors often make: They pay taxes on other people's income and capital gains. How do they accomplish that astonishing feat? By buying shares just before income and capital gains distributions. Most parts of the tax code have at least some semblance of being fair. But this one doesn't.

Assume for a moment that you invest $10,000 in a fund and a few days later that fund declares its annual capital gains distribution. After a good year, that distribution could amount to 10 percent of the fund's value, or $1,000 in this hypothetical case. Assuming you have the distribution reinvested in the fund, you are in exactly the same position that you were before the distribution. You have more shares, but each share is worth less.

But then along comes Uncle Sam, who says that $1,000 distribution is a capital gain on which you must pay taxes. Even though it was your own money that was paid back to you, the law says it's taxable income. If you pay at a 15 percent capital gains rate, this will cost you $150. To pay the tax, you must either sell some of your fund shares or use other money. The latter option effectively increases your cost without giving you any benefit.

This is a very annoying leak that you can avoid. Here's how: Before you make a sizeable investment in a mutual fund inside a taxable account, inquire about any upcoming distributions. If you can postpone your purchase until right after the distribution, you'll avoid this tax hit. This isn't difficult. It's an excellent example of an important lesson I hope you take away from this chapter: Investors who pay attention to details are much less likely to part with their money unknowingly. Getting the details right is one of the most reliable ways I know to say goodbye to anxiety and say hello to peace of mind, to wind up with more money along with more time and energy to pursue things that matter most in your life.

## Variable Annuities

A variable annuity is a contract between an investor and an insurance company. It allows a portfolio of investments to accumulate on a tax-deferred basis. Variable annuities are terrific if you are producing them (insurance companies) or selling them (insurance agents and other planners). But if you're buying them, they are usually a lethal combination of too-high expenses and too-high taxes.

Variable annuity expenses are notoriously high. A few years back, Morningstar reported that the annual expenses charged by the average domestic stock subaccount (equivalent to a mutual fund) in its variable annuity database were 2.1 percent. That was nearly twice the 1.1 percent charged by the average no-load mutual fund—and 20 times as much as some index funds.

Part of the charge is for life insurance that most likely will be worthless even as it increases in cost. That sounds harsh, but here's how it works: The insurance premium you pay is calculated each year as a percentage of your

*(Continued)*

total account balance. If the value of your account doubles, your premium will double.

But this insurance typically guarantees only that if you die, your heirs will receive at least as much as you originally invested. As long as your account is worth more than your initial investment, the insurance company won't ever have to pay on this insurance. This has to be the most profitable insurance any company can sell. As the company's risk goes down (with every dollar you make), the premiums it collects go up. If that doesn't add up to a rotten deal for investors, I don't know what would.

Annuities usually require investors who want their money back to pay surrender charges or liquidation penalties for so-called early withdrawals, typically in the first six to 10 years of the contract. That sacrifices liquidity, the ability to get your money back from an investment when you need it. In addition, the IRS adds penalties for investors who take their money out before age 59½.

While most variable annuities offer several investment options, usually the asset classes available are quite limited, and most are actively managed funds. This means it's impossible for investors to make their money work very hard.

It's ironic that variable annuities are promoted as tax shelters. If most people understood the details, they'd never invest. There are three main tax flaws with variable annuities:

1. Money you put into them isn't tax-deductible.
2. All earnings in the account are eventually taxed as ordinary income at the investor's highest tax bracket. When you buy a variable annuity, you say goodbye to the benefits of the 15 percent cap on tax rates for dividends and capital gains. The tax rate you pay can be more than twice that high.
3. Even though you may have a substantial tax basis in the account, when you start living off your annuity savings, all your withdrawals will be considered income (on which you must pay tax at your top rate) until you've withdrawn 100 percent of your earnings. Only then will you be able to withdraw your original investment tax-free. By that time, you're likely to feel that you've been taxed to the max.

Here's my bottom-line advice on variable annuities: Don't buy one unless you have read the entire contract and you're sure that you understand every paragraph. Furthermore, if any insurance agent or adviser tells you to put a variable annuity inside an IRA or other tax shelter, immediately terminate the conversation. This is a sure sign in my opinion that your best interests are not being treated as the most important ones.

If you already own a variable annuity, or if you decide you are one of the exceptions for whom a variable annuity is the right product, do what's known as a Section 1035 exchange and move the assets into a low-cost, no-commission annuity through Vanguard or Dimensional Fund Advisors, where you at least won't be hemmed in by stiff early redemption penalties.

For a more complete discussion of this topic, see the article "All About Annuities" at FundAdvice.com

CHAPTER 12

# Putting Your Ideal
# Portfolio to Work

*Genius is the ability to put into effect what is in your mind.*
—F. Scott Fitzgerald

If you have followed the sequence of learning and thinking and evaluating the steps in this book so far, by this time you know what kinds of assets are likely to maximize your chances of investment success while keeping your risk under control. The question at this point is purely practical: Where is the very best place to put your money so you get the assets you need?

You know you should use no-load mutual funds and that you should diversify widely among the right asset classes. You know you should do all you can to minimize your expenses and taxes. There are many places you can invest your money to get an adequate return. But there's no reason you should settle for an okay portfolio when you can have a great portfolio.

This chapter shows you several ways to go from okay to great. None is perfect, but any one of them can be a low-cost ticket to successful, tax-efficient investing.

A number of no-load mutual fund families offer low-cost funds that are definitely a cut above the ordinary. For investors with 401(k) plans run by T. Rowe Price,

Fidelity, or Vanguard—and for other investors who for whatever reason want to keep their money at one of those companies—our suggested portfolios show how to take maximum advantage of that opportunity.

For taxable accounts, there are excellent funds specifically managed to reduce your income tax bite, leaving more of the portfolios' growth and income for you and less for Uncle Sam.

If you want the very best assets at the lowest cost and with the highest tax efficiency, check out our "ultimate equity portfolio" of funds from Dimensional Fund Advisors (DFA). These funds are off-limits to do-it-yourself investors—they are available only through investment advisers. Some people regard that as a drawback, because investment advisers charge management fees and have account size minimums. However, as you will see in Chapter 14, there is much value in having an adviser.

In some ways, this is the most daunting chapter in this book, because it's full of tables and comparisons of many kinds. Here's a quick guide to the parts that might be of immediate interest:

This chapter presents specific recommendations for investors enrolled in 401(k) plans run by T. Rowe Price, Fidelity, and Vanguard. Along with our ultimate equity portfolio, you'll find a discussion of what makes DFA funds superior.

A series of tables compares the funds of Vanguard and DFA with the averages of their peers as tracked by Morningstar.

Finally, we point you to a web site where you can find suggested portfolios for retirement plans that use funds from Schwab, TIAA-CREFF, and others, as well as our specific recommendations for 401(k) and similar plans run by many large employers.

**M**ost investors, for various reasons, wind up with portfolios that almost by default are heavily overweighted in large U.S. growth stocks. Historically, this asset class has had the lowest long-term performance since 1926 of all those we recommend.

As you know from earlier chapters in this book, investors who want to make their money work hard for them must go far beyond the most popular funds. Fortunately, there are a number of ways to do this.

*Exchange-traded funds* (ETFs) have become an increasingly popular vehicle. Because they don't have minimum initial investment requirements, ETFs give small investors a super-low-cost way to gain access to many asset classes. Most are based on stock indexes, making them tax efficient and exempt from the costs (and likely underperformance) of active management.

As their name implies, these funds are traded on stock exchanges. They can be bought and sold during market hours at whatever the market price is at any moment. (By contrast, mutual funds can be bought and sold only once a day, and they have only one price, set at the market's close.) ETFs also can be sold short or purchased on margin.

These attributes make ETFs convenient for traders. One important downside of ETFs is that they can't be bought or sold without paying a brokerage commission. This commission is usually a small number of dollars, and for large purchases it amounts to a tiny fraction of the purchase or sales price. However, the sales commission can be a deterrent to periodic rebalancing, an important step in keeping risks under control. For more discussion of ETFs and my company's specific recommendations, go to FundAdvice.com and find an article called "The Truth about ETFs."

*T. Rowe Price* is a venerable and respected no-load fund family known for conservative management, wide diversification, and reasonable expenses. You won't often find these funds at the very top of performance lists, but you'll almost never find them near the bottom, either. Nor will you find gimmick funds here. T. Rowe Price by and large stays with the tried-and-true. (See Table 12.1.)

*Fidelity* is the powerhouse of 401(k) plans, and millions of employees depend on Fidelity funds for important parts of their retirement savings. Fidelity has a deep, highly respected pool of securities analysts and offers a huge variety of funds with specialized portfolios, most of which investors don't really need. The company does an above-average job of keeping its costs reasonable, offering some index funds with extremely low expense ratios.

However, many of the 401(k) plans put together by Fidelity are dominated by the company's large-cap U.S. funds, depriving many

**Table 12.1    T. Rowe Price Suggested Portfolio (All Equity)**

| Fund | Asset Class | Percentage | Ticker |
|------|-------------|------------|--------|
| Equity Index 500 | U.S. large-cap blend | 10% | PREIX |
| Value | U.S. large-cap value | 10% | TRVLX |
| Diversified Small-Cap Growth | U.S. small-cap growth | 20% | PRDSX |
| Real Estate | U.S. real estate | 10% | TRREX |
| International Equity Index | International large-cap | 10% | PIEQX |
| International Growth & Income | International large-cap value | 10% | TRIGX |
| International Discovery | International small-cap growth | 20% | PRIDX |
| Emerging Market Stock | Emerging markets | 10% | PRMSX |

investors of access to asset classes that could enhance their diversification. If you are a participant in such a plan, I suggest you contact your plan trustees and request more choices. You can find suggestions on how to do that at 401khelp.com.

Table 12.2 shows our Fidelity suggested portfolio.

(*Note:* The portfolios we show here are all-equity, but I believe most investors should have a fixed-income component as well. You'll find fixed-income recommendations for each of our portfolios online at FundAdvice.com.)

**Table 12.2    Fidelity Suggested Equity Portfolio**

| Fund | Asset Class | Percentage | Ticker |
|------|-------------|------------|--------|
| Spartan 500 Index | U.S. large-cap blend | 10% | FSMKX |
| Structured Large-Cap Value | U.S. large-cap value | 10% | FSLVX |
| Small-Cap Independence | U.S. small-cap growth | 10% | FDSCX |
| Small-Cap Value | U.S. small-cap value | 10% | FCPVX |
| Real Estate | U.S. real estate | 10% | FRESX |
| Spartan International Index | International large-cap | 10% | FSIIX |
| International Value | International large-cap value | 10% | FIVLX |
| International Small-Cap Opportunity | International small-cap growth | 20% | FSCOX |
| Emerging Markets | Emerging markets | 10% | FEMKX |

*Vanguard* has for many years been our favorite source of low-cost, tax-efficient index funds for do-it-yourself investors. Unfortunately, Vanguard in 2004 closed its International Explorer Fund (VINEX) to new accounts, locking new investors out of international small-cap stocks. However, some 401(k) plans still provide access to this fund; if it's available to you, I think you should take advantage of it. Table 12.3 shows our Vanguard suggested portfolio.

Each of these portfolios is convenient, consisting of funds from a single family that can be held in one account. But none of those portfolios covers all the bases. For investors who don't want to compromise on asset classes, I offer the Merriman Model Portfolio, which you can find online at FundAdvice.com. This group of no-load funds is the best bet for do-it-yourself investors who are willing to go anywhere and who can accept the inconvenience of multiple fund families and multiple statements. Many of these funds may be available through Schwab and other discount brokerages, so it may not be necessary to have as many accounts as this list would suggest.

All the portfolios I have outlined are good ways for you to build Your Ideal Portfolio using low-cost, tax-efficient, no-load funds. If you own a portfolio like that and rebalance it each year, adding money as you can, you will probably be among the most successful long-term investors.

However, I'm committed to giving you the very best possible advice, and that compels me to introduce what I call "the best mutual funds in the world." That's not a description I would ever use casually, but I believe it's accurate.

**Table 12.3    Vanguard Suggested Equity Portfolio**

| Fund | Asset Class | Percentage | Ticker |
|---|---|---|---|
| 500 Index | U.S. large-cap blend | 10% | VFINX |
| Value Index | U.S. large-cap value | 10% | VIVAX |
| Small-Cap Index | U.S. small-cap growth | 10% | NAESX |
| Small-Cap Value Index | U.S. small-cap value | 10% | VISVX |
| REIT Index | U.S. real estate | 10% | VGSIX |
| Developed Markets Index | International large-cap | 20% | VDMIX |
| International Value | International large-cap value | 20% | VTRIX |
| Emerging Market Index | Emerging markets | 10% | VEIEX |

In a quarter-century of managing money for clients, the best way I've ever found to build a portfolio is using the no-load asset-class funds offered by Dimensional Fund Advisors (DFA). These funds were specifically created to help investors pinpoint the most productive types of assets, as identified by the academic research that underlies what we call Your Ideal Portfolio.

Dimensional Fund Advisors funds have a couple of drawbacks. First, they are available only through investment advisers, whose management fees are normally around 1 percent annually. Second, advisers who offer these funds normally have minimum account sizes of $100,000 or more. But for investors who can get past those hurdles, I believe DFA funds will provide the extra edge over time that will make them great investments instead of just good ones.

Without further ado, let's look at what I consider the ultimate equity portfolio (Table 12.4). As a portfolio, I'll put this combination up against any similarly weighted funds in the same asset classes.

It's interesting to compare the ultimate equity portfolio with our Vanguard suggested portfolio. We can make that comparison back to 1999, when the Vanguard U.S. Small-Cap Value Fund came on the scene. Table 12.5 shows that year-by-year comparison.

As you can see, the ultimate equity portfolio of DFA funds did much better in all but one year. The critical question is why—and whether that advantage is something investors can reasonably expect in the future.

**Table 12.4    The Ultimate Suggested Equity Portfolio**

| Fund (All Are DFA) | Asset Class | Percentage | Ticker |
|---|---|---|---|
| U.S. Large Company | U.S. large-cap blend | 10% | DFLCX |
| U.S. Large Cap Value | U.S. large-cap value | 10% | DFLVX |
| U.S. Micro Cap | U.S. small-cap | 10% | DFSCX |
| U.S. Small Cap Value | U.S. small-cap value | 10% | DFSVX |
| U.S. REITs | U.S. real estate | 10% | DFREX |
| International Large Cap | International large-cap | 10% | DFALX |
| International Large Cap Value | International large-cap value | 10% | DFIVX |
| International Small Cap | International small-cap | 10% | DFISX |
| International Small Cap Value | International small-cap value | 10% | DISVX |
| Emerging Markets Core Equity | Emerging markets | 10% | DFCEX |

**Table 12.5  Vanguard Suggested Portfolio versus Ultimate Equity Portfolio, 1999–2007**

| Year | Vanguard | Ultimate |
|------|----------|----------|
| 1999 | 21.5% | 23.0% |
| 2000 | −2.8% | −1.9% |
| 2001 | −7.0% | −0.5% |
| 2002 | −13.9% | −7.6% |
| 2003 | 39.8% | 49.8% |
| 2004 | 20.6% | 25.0% |
| 2005 | 13.2% | 14.5% |
| 2006 | 24.4% | 25.2% |
| 2007 | 6.8% | 3.7% |

Dimensional Fund Advisors' superior performance is not the result of better managers picking better stocks. Stock picking plays only a very minor role in these funds, which are passively managed. DFA funds' edge comes from precise asset allocations that give investors more of what they need and less of what they don't need.

To demonstrate this, let's compare Vanguard's large-cap U.S. value fund (Vanguard Value Index Fund) with DFA's comparable fund (DFA Large Company Value Fund). Statistically, the DFA fund has a much stronger concentration of value, according to a measurement known as the price-to-book (P/B) ratio.

Imagine that growth versus value is represented by a straight line across a page, with pure value at the far left and pure growth at the far right. Statistically, we can measure the orientation along this line for a mutual fund portfolio. Most funds fall somewhere on the line between the extremes of growth and value.

I don't believe investors need to analyze individual stocks, but in order to understand value, I invite you into the following discussion. Most experts on asset allocation look at growth versus value in two ways. First, they consider that low price/earnings (P/E) ratios represent value and high P/E ratios represent growth. Second, and the measure we'll use for our discussion since it is regarded by academics as the best measure of value, is the price/book (P/B) ratio of a stock. This ratio indicates how much investors are willing to pay in relation to a company's book value per share. Book value consists of the cash and all other assets on a company's books, minus all liabilities.

A low P/B ratio suggests that investors place a high importance on physical assets. A high P/B ratio indicates investors think something else is more important, most likely a company's ability to generate future profits. At Google, for example, the company's physical assets and cash hoard are valuable, but they are only incidental in comparison with the brainpower of the company's workforce.

Imagine a company that is facing enormous challenges such as heavy debts, faltering management, and perhaps other serious problems like lawsuits, government crackdowns, or competitors with products that could make this company's products obsolete. In an extreme case, investors might be so unenthusiastic about such a company that the share price could be less than the fire-sale value of the assets in the event that the company was liquidated. That would make it a highly discounted value stock.

If the share price were equal to the book value, for a P/B ratio of 1.0, investors would be saying in effect that the company is worth only the balance sheet value of its buildings, land, trucks, equipment, computers, inventory, cash, and all the other assets on its books, minus the liabilities. That stock price would place no value at all on the company's ability to use those assets to generate profits.

That's an extreme example, and most stocks in value funds are not in terrible trouble, only out of favor for various reasons.

The S&P 500 Index, generally regarded as having a portfolio that represents a midpoint between value and growth, has a P/B ratio of 2.4 as this is being written. (The number goes up and down with stock market cycles. The figure is always readily accessible at Morningstar.com on the portfolio page for the Vanguard 500 Index Fund.) For this discussion, let's regard a P/B ratio of 2.4 as neutral, representing neither growth nor value.

The P/B ratio of the DFA Large Company Value Fund is 1.5. By contrast, Vanguard's Growth Index Fund (VIGRX), has a P/B ratio of 3.4.

When you're trying to capture the benefit of investing in value companies, you will get more of that benefit from funds that invest in companies with lower P/B ratios.

Table 12.6 shows the P/B ratios of the U.S. large-cap value funds in the portfolios we have listed in this chapter. Table 12.7 shows annual (and cumulative) performance for the same four funds for 2001 through 2007.

These numbers reflect only a few years. But the DFA fund's greater orientation to value makes it a much better way to gain the advantage of value investing that we saw in Chapter 8. In Your Ideal Portfolio, value works best when it is clearly differentiated from the

**Table 12.6  Price/Book Ratios of U.S. Large-Cap Value Funds**

| Fund | Price/Book Ratio |
| --- | --- |
| T. Rowe Price Value | 2.0 |
| Fidelity Equity Income | 1.9 |
| Vanguard Value Index | 2.2 |
| DFA Large Company Value | 1.5 |

**Table 12.7  Performance of U.S. Large-Cap Value Funds**

| Fund | 2001 | 2002 | 2003 | 2004 | 2005 | 2006 | 2007 | $10,000 Grew to |
| --- | --- | --- | --- | --- | --- | --- | --- | --- |
| T. Rowe Price Value | 1.6% | −16.6% | 30.0% | 15.4% | 6.3% | 19.8% | 0.8% | $16,318 |
| Fidelity Equity Income | −5.0% | −17.2% | 30.0% | 11.3% | 5.7% | 19.8% | 1.4% | $14,614 |
| Vanguard Value Index | −11.9% | −20.9% | 32.3% | 15.3% | 7.1% | 22.2% | 0.1% | $13,926 |
| DFA Large Company Value | 3.8% | −14.9% | 34.4% | 18.3% | 10.2% | 20.2% | −2.8% | $18,083 |

overall market. And DFA's fund does that better than any comparable fund I know.

Let's look also at the size factor. To get the full advantage from investing in small-cap companies, you should own really *small* companies, not just those at the lower end of the mid-cap category.

Again, you can imagine a spectrum from tiny companies with total market capitalization under $50 million to giants like ExxonMobil Corp ($475 billion). Although there are no hard-and-fast definitions, small-cap stocks are generally regarded as those with market caps of $1.5 billion or less.

Over the very long term, I believe that smaller is better, and some funds give investors more smallness than others. That is pointedly the case with the DFA U.S. Micro Cap Fund. In a year when all stocks do well and small-cap stocks do better, the DFA fund should shine. Such a year was 2003. The returns that year for four U.S. small-cap funds are shown in Table 12.8; for each fund, I've

**Table 12.8   Four U.S. Small-Cap Funds, 2003**

| Fund | 2003 | Median Market Capitalization (Thousands) | Stocks in Portfolio |
|---|---|---|---|
| T. Rowe Price Diversified Small-Cap Growth | 40.2% | $1,382,000 | 291 |
| Fidelity Small-Cap Stock | 45.0% | $871,000 | 249 |
| Vanguard Small-Cap Index | 45.6% | $1,198,000 | 1,748 |
| DFA U.S. Micro Cap | 60.7% | $279,000 | 2,494 |

also included the median market capitalization of its portfolio and the total number of stock holdings.

The DFA size advantage is not an accident. The company's U.S. Micro Cap Fund invests only in the smallest 20 percent of all U.S. stocks—technically the 9th and 10th deciles based on the size of companies on the New York Stock Exchange.

In years when smaller stocks are faring worse than average, the effect works in reverse and DFA returns will be hit harder. Should that deter you from investing in the DFA funds? I don't think so, and here's why: Over the long term, investors usually receive premium returns for taking carefully controlled risks. Investing in a broadly diversified portfolio of very small companies represents a carefully controlled risk that is likely to give investors a premium return.

So far we have seen two main advantages of DFA funds: They deliver smaller smallness and more deeply discounted value. DFA funds also excel in a third way: They have low portfolio turnover, which allows them to be more cost-efficient and more tax-efficient than even index funds.

Funds that track specific indexes must buy and sell periodically whenever the stocks in an index change. The purchases and sales usually coincide with the purchases and sales of every other fund that tracks the same index. It's hard to get the best price when many other big buyers (or sellers) are doing the same thing you are. When an index fund updates its portfolio semiannually, this can cost two to four percentage points of return.

DFA funds are not strictly index funds, and therefore they are not obligated to buy and sell stocks except to keep their portfolios representative of their asset classes. Table 12.9 shows the annual

**Table 12.9   Comparison of Annual Portfolio Turnover in Four Asset Classes**

| Fund Family | U.S. Large Value | U.S. Small-Cap | International Large-Cap | Emerging Markets |
|---|---|---|---|---|
| T. Rowe Price | 10% | 39% | 36% | 49% |
| Fidelity | 24% | 126% | 2% | 66% |
| Vanguard | 20% | 24% | 9% | 26% |
| Dimensional Fund Advisors | 9% | 24% | 4% | 6% |

portfolio turnover for 2007 of four funds each in three asset classes, from the portfolios listed earlier.

In almost every case, DFA funds had lower portfolio turnover than the actively managed funds and index funds. This doesn't guarantee higher returns, but it stacks the odds in the investor's favor by plugging a large potential leak.

Investors should focus on what they can control and try not to worry too much about what they can't control. The most important thing investors can control is the kind of assets they put in their portfolios. More than anything else, that determines their returns.

I'm including a series of tables (Tables 12.10 through 12.17) that show why I believe Vanguard and DFA funds are superior. Listing individual funds in 10 equity asset classes, the tables compare Vanguard and DFA against each other and against the category averages compiled by Morningstar.

The final moment of truth for serious investors is whether it makes sense to hire an investment adviser in order to get access to DFA funds. For many years I have preached the gospel of low-cost investing. I don't want you to pay a penny more for your investments than you have to. But neither do I want you to be penny-wise and pound-foolish.

My company's studies indicate that over time, DFA funds should have an advantage of at least one percentage point a year over Vanguard funds, even after the effect of a presumed 1 percent annual management fee. This net advantage can make the difference between retiring when you want to or having to work longer. It can make the difference between running out of money or not. It can make the difference between retiring with a substantial cushion or having to just get by.

**Table 12.10   Comparison of Expenses, Vanguard versus DFA versus Category**

(Lower number is desirable)

| Asset Class | Dimension | Vanguard | Category Average |
|---|---|---|---|
| U.S. large-cap | 0.15% | 0.18% | 1.11% |
| U.S. large-cap value | 0.28% | 0.21% | 1.29% |
| U.S. micro-cap | 0.53% | 0.23% | 1.38% |
| U.S. small-cap value | 0.53% | 0.23% | 1.50% |
| U.S. REITs* | 0.33% | 0.21% | 1.46% |
| International large-cap* | 0.29% | 0.22% | 1.44% |
| International large-cap value* | 0.44% | 0.45% | 1.41% |
| International small-cap* | 0.56% | 0.43% | 1.65% |
| International small-cap value | 0.70% | None | 1.56% |
| Emerging markets (Core for DFA)* | 0.74% | 0.42% | 1.82% |
| **Average** | **1.46%** | **0.29%** | **1.46%** |

* Vanguard applies: redemption fee: 1% if held < 1 year for Reits fund.
Redemption fee: 2% if held < 2 months for Developed Markets fund.
Redemption fee: 2% if held < 2 months for International Value fund.
Redemption fee: 2% if held < 2 months for International Explorer fund.
Purchase fee: 0.5%, redemption fee: 0.5% for Emerging Market fund.

**Table 12.11   Average market capitalizations: DFA versus Vanguard versus Morningstar category averages**

(Lower number is desirable)    In millions

| Asset Class | Dimensional | Vanguard | Category Average |
|---|---|---|---|
| U.S. large-cap | $55,115 | $57,539 | $42,566 |
| U.S. large-cap value | $19,491 | $58,388 | $47,126 |
| U.S. micro-cap | $435 | $1,699 | $1,351 |
| U.S. small-cap value | $761 | $1,602 | $1,147 |
| U.S. Reits | $5,969 | $5,833 | $6,438 |
| International large-cap | $34,718 | $37,556 | $32,765 |
| International large-cap value | $30,158 | $44,532 | $33,302 |
| International small-cap | $926 | $1,969 | $3,649 |
| International small-cap value | $903 | – | $3,363 |
| Emerging markets | $6,189 | $18,735 | $16,095 |
| **Average** | **$15,467** | **$25,317** | **$18,780** |

**Table 12.12   Value Orientation Average price/book ratios: DFA versus Vanguard versus Category Averages**

(lower number is desirable)

| Asset Class | Dimensional | Vanguard | Category Average |
|---|---|---|---|
| U.S. large-cap | 2.9 | 2.9 | 2.9 |
| U.S. large-cap value | 1.5 | 2.2 | 2.4 |
| U.S. micro-cap | 2.1 | 2.3 | 2.3 |
| U.S. small-cap value | 1.3 | 1.7 | 1.8 |
| U.S. REITs | 2.7 | 2.6 | 2.4 |
| International large-cap | 3.0 | 3.0 | 3.3 |
| International large-cap value | 2.2 | 2.9 | 2.5 |
| International small-cap | 2.3 | 2.7 | 3.4 |
| International small-cap value | 1.3 | – | 2.8 |
| Emerging markets (Core for DFA) | 2.7 | 3.2 | 3.7 |
| **Average** | **2.2** | **2.6** | **2.75** |

**Table 12.13   Turnover Ratio: DFA versus Vanguard versus Morningstar Category Averages**

(lower number is desirable)

| Asset Class | Dimensional | Vanguard | Category Average |
|---|---|---|---|
| U.S. large-cap | 6.0% | 5.0% | 71.0% |
| U.S. large-cap value | 9.0% | 20.0% | 57.0% |
| U.S. micro-cap | 24.0% | 24.0% | 85.0% |
| U.S. small-cap value | 27.0% | 25.0% | 73.0% |
| U.S. Reits | 10.0% | 21.0% | 76.0% |
| International large-cap | 4.0% | 7.0% | 73.0% |
| International large-cap value | 15.0% | 38.0% | 50.0% |
| International small-cap | 11.0% | 45.0% | 66.0% |
| International small-cap value | 14.0% | – | 57.0% |
| Emerging markets (Core for DFA) | 6.0% | 9.0% | 76.0% |
| **Average** | **12.6%** | **21.6%** | **68.4%** |

**Table 12.14** **Stocks held in portfolios: DFA versus Vanguard versus Morningstar Category Averages**

(higher number is desirable)

| Asset Class | Dimensional | Vanguard | Category average |
|---|---|---|---|
| U.S. large-cap | 502 | 512 | 232 |
| U.S. large-cap value | 249 | 395 | 100 |
| U.S. micro-cap | 2,404 | 1,691 | 379 |
| U.S. small-cap value | 1,330 | 922 | 224 |
| U.S. Reits | 104 | 100 | 70 |
| International large-cap | 1,689 | 1,244 | 261 |
| International large-cap value | 599 | 223 | 124 |
| International small-cap | 4,574 | 233 | 280 |
| International small-cap value | 2,487 | – | 373 |
| Emerging markets | 2,525 | 845 | 207 |
| **Average** | **1,646** | **685** | **225** |

**Table 12.15** **Comparison of One-Year Returns, Vanguard versus DFA versus Category, 2007**

| Asset Class | Dimensional | Vanguard | Category Average |
|---|---|---|---|
| U.S. large-cap | 5.4% | 5.4% | 6.2% |
| U.S. large-cap value | −2.8% | 0.1% | 1.4% |
| U.S. micro-cap | −5.2% | 1.2% | −1.1% |
| U.S. small-cap value | −10.7% | −7.1% | −6.1% |
| U.S. REITs | −18.7% | −16.5% | −14.7% |
| International large-cap | 12.5% | 11.0% | 12.7% |
| International large-cap value | 10.2% | 12.7% | 9.0% |
| International small-cap | 5.7% | 5.2% | 8.5% |
| International small-cap value | 2.9% | – | 5.0% |
| Emerging markets | 37.5% | 37.5% | 36.7% |
| **Average** | **3.68%** | **5.49%** | **5.77%** |

**Table 12.16** **Comparison of Five-Year Returns, Vanguard versus DFA versus Category, 2003–2007**

| Asset Class | Dimensional | Vanguard | Category Average |
|---|---|---|---|
| U.S. large-cap | 12.7% | 12.7% | 12.6% |
| U.S. large-cap value | 15.4% | 14.8% | 13.2% |
| U.S. micro-cap | 17.2% | 17.0% | 15.7% |
| U.S. small-cap value | 18.5% | 14.8% | 14.6% |
| U.S. REITs | 17.4% | 17.5% | 17.7% |
| International large-cap | 20.9% | 21.5% | 20.3% |
| International large-cap value | 26.9% | 23.5% | 20.9% |
| International small-cap | 27.3% | 27.9% | 25.9% |
| International small-cap value | 29.6% | – | 23.7% |
| Emerging markets | 36.6% | 36.4% | 32.5% |
| **Average** | **22.3%** | **20.7%** | **20.0%** |

**Table 12.17** **Comparison of Five-Year Tax-Adjusted Returns, Vanguard versus DFA versus Category, 2003–2007**

| Asset Class | Dimensional | Vanguard | Category Average |
|---|---|---|---|
| U.S. large-cap | 12.0% | 12.4% | 11.6% |
| U.S. large-cap value | 14.6% | 14.4% | 11.6% |
| U.S. micro-cap | 15.7% | 16.8% | 13.9% |
| U.S. small-cap value | 16.8% | 14.3% | 12.4% |
| U.S. REITs | 15.5% | 15.5% | 14.7% |
| International large-cap | 19.9% | 20.9% | 19.0% |
| International large-cap value | 25.5% | 22.4% | 19.1% |
| International small-cap | 25.7% | 26.6% | 23.8% |
| International small-cap value | 27.8% | – | 21.3% |
| Emerging markets | 35.4% | 36.1% | 33.0% |
| **Average** | **20.9%** | **19.9%** | **18.0%** |

Many investors are reluctant to pay for a manager's services. But I hope you won't veto the idea out of hand. What if you had a high probability of making more money with an adviser than without one? In Chapter 14 you will find some statistics from Morningstar that I regard as compelling evidence that DFA funds provide ample rewards for paying the management fees necessary to gain access to them.

## Tax-Managed Funds

Fidelity's and Vanguard's index funds are extremely tax efficient, as are the asset-class funds of DFA. Still, there's another level of tax efficiency that's available to investors in high tax brackets: Both Vanguard and DFA have excellent funds that are specifically managed to minimize the tax leaks from income and capital gains distributions.

What's a tax-managed fund? Two nearly identical Vanguard U.S. large-cap blend funds provide a good example, based on our discussion in Chapter 11 of tax-adjusted returns. I'd like to compare the Vanguard 500 Index Fund with the Vanguard Tax-Managed Growth & Income Fund. The first is managed without regard to taxes, while the second is designed to minimize the taxes that shareholders must pay.

The expense ratios of these funds are essentially the same (0.18 percent for 500 Index, 0.15 percent for the tax-managed fund), and their portfolios have identical risk levels, according to Morningstar. The stocks in these two funds are usually identical or nearly so. But the managers make trades in the tax-managed fund to realize capital losses in order to offset realized gains. This means the tax-managed fund will sometimes stray slightly from the index.

When we looked late in 2007, their 10-year returns (before the effect of taxes) were within 0.1 percentage point of each other. The same was true of their returns over the most recent one, three, and five years—and in every case the tax-managed fund's return was the higher one.

When the results are adjusted to reflect taxes that investors in the highest tax brackets would have paid during the 10 years ending October 31, 2007, the tax-adjusted annual return was 7.02 percent for the Vanguard 500 Index Fund and 7.11 percent for the Vanguard Tax-Managed Growth & Income Fund. On a $10,000 investment over 10 years, that's the difference between $19,708 and $19,875. Although that difference is small, it's an edge that's purposeful and predictable, one more way investors can stack the odds in their favor.

Not every asset class is represented by a tax-managed fund, but several are. When we design a portfolio for somebody in a high tax bracket, we use our same basic portfolios but substitute tax-managed funds when we can. Table 12.18 shows our Vanguard tax-managed suggested portfolio.

**Table 12.18 Vanguard Tax-Managed Suggested Equity Portfolio**

| Fund | Asset Class | Percentage | Ticker |
|------|-------------|------------|--------|
| Tax-Managed Growth | U.S. large-cap blend | 12.5% | VTGIX |
| Value Index | U.S. large-cap value | 12.5% | VIVAX |
| Small-Cap Index | U.S. small-cap growth | 12.5% | NAESX |
| Small-Cap Value Index | U.S. small-cap value | 12.5% | VISVX |
| Tax-Managed International | International large-cap | 20.0% | VDMIX |
| International Value | International large-cap value | 20.0% | VTRIX |
| Emerging Market Index | Emerging markets | 10.0% | VEIEX |

Vanguard's other tax-managed funds include the Tax-Managed Balanced Fund and the Tax-Managed Capital Appreciation Fund. DFA has five tax-managed funds: the Tax-Managed U.S. Equity Fund, the Tax-Managed U.S. Marketwide Value Fund, the Tax-Managed U.S. Small-Cap Fund, the Tax-Managed Small-Cap Value Fund, and the Tax-Managed International Value Fund. Table 12.19 shows how we would modify the ultimate equity portfolio for the most tax-efficient strategy using those funds.

**Table 12.19 The Ultimate Tax-Managed Suggested Equity Portfolio**

| Fund (All DFA) | Asset Class | Percentage | Ticker |
|----------------|-------------|------------|--------|
| Tax-Managed U.S. Equity | U.S. large-cap blend | 12.5% | DTMEX |
| Tax-Managed U.S. Marketwide Value | U.S. large-cap value | 12.5% | DTMMX |
| Tax-Managed U.S. Small Cap | U.S. small-cap growth | 12.5% | DFTSX |
| Tax-Managed U.S. Small Cap Value | U.S. small-cap value | 12.5% | DTMVX |
| International Large Company | International large-cap | 10.0% | DFALX |
| Tax-Managed International Value | International large-cap value | 10.0% | DTMIX |
| International Small | International small-cap | 10.0% | DFISX |
| International Small Value | International small-cap value | 10.0% | DISVX |
| Emerging Markets Core Equity | Emerging markets | 10.0% | DFCEX |

*(Continued)*

> Tax-managed funds don't cover every important asset class, so they can't make up all of a properly diversified portfolio. But adding even a few of them makes a noticeable difference, especially at tax time.

## Further Resources

This chapter has focused on specific recommendations that will be suitable for many investors. But there are many other good ways to put together a portfolio, especially if you are in an employer-sponsored plan or for some reason need to keep your investments consolidated in one place.

At my company's educational web site, FundAdvice.com, you'll always find the up-to-date versions of the portfolios I have introduced here. In addition, we have suggested portfolios for investors who use exchange-traded funds plus portfolios of mutual funds for investors at Schwab, Etrade, Firstrade, and TD Ameritrade.

You'll also find portfolio suggestions suitable for emergency funds and monthly income.

The portfolios in this chapter are all in equities. I've done that for simplicity's sake, not because I think investors should ignore fixed-income funds. On the contrary, as I've indicated in previous chapters, fixed-income is an extremely important part of most portfolios.

At FundAdvice.com, you'll find balanced portfolios for all the major fund families and brokerage houses, each one predicated on the 60/40 split we have used as a basis for the discussion in this book. If the right split for you is something other than 60/40, you (or an adviser if you use one) will be able to easily convert the percentages that we are recommending to fit your needs.

This web site also has a unique resource for the millions of working investors who are accumulating assets through 401(k) and similar plans. At 401khelp.com (that's how you can get to this part of the web site directly), my company has analyzed more than 80 corporate and government employer plans. You'll find specific recommendations based on the available options in each plan.

These include quite a few small companies as well as giant corporations like Microsoft, General Motors, Boeing, American Airlines,

Bank of America, IBM, Merck, and Wells Fargo. Also on the site are recommendations for the giant U.S. government Thrift Savings Plan as well as many state, city, university, and nonprofit plans.

With all these resources, I hope you can see there are many fine ways to make your money work hard for you. If you take advantage of them, you'll be much more likely to live it up in retirement. I hope you do so.

# CHAPTER 13

# Withdrawals

## WHEN YOUR PORTFOLIO STARTS PAYING YOU

*It is better to live rich than to die rich.*

—Samuel Johnson

This chapter could be called "The Facts of Life for Retirees." It gets right to the nub of some choices that cannot be avoided. There are very few financial changes as important as retirement. It's the end of paying your portfolio and the start of having your portfolio pay you. How you go about this transition will have financial repercussions for the rest of your life—and most likely for your heirs after you are gone.

You may have saved for many years and invested your money carefully. But when the money has to flow in the reverse direction, suddenly you face four major decisions that will determine the bulk of your financial future.

1. How will you invest your money?
2. How much risk will you take?
3. How much do you need or want regularly from your portfolio?
4. Do you need a fixed income or can you tolerate a variable income?

The first two questions are related, and they're addressed in detail in Chapters 6 through 9. We discussed the third question in Chapter 5. I repeat those questions here because the answers may be different for retirees than for pre-retirees. Thus, those topics may be worth revisiting.

This chapter is concerned with the fourth question and the implications of various possible answers to it.

The biggest financial risk retirees face is running out of money before they run out of life. How you structure your withdrawals plays a major role in this. This topic is necessarily full of numbers, tables, percentages, projections, and assumptions, all of them very important. But the subject of withdrawals can be emotional and challenging beyond the math. If ever there is a time in a person's financial life when the rubber finally meets the road, this is it. In a way, this step is a sort of final salary negotiation between retirees and their portfolios.

One of my clients, after I had counseled him and his wife on the subject of how much they were spending, angrily accused me of causing a rift between the two of them. In fact, what I had done was raise issues that they needed to address early in their retirement. If they hadn't done that, they might have one day faced a crisis and been forced to deal with these issues later, when the stakes would have been higher and their options much more limited.

This chapter seems to be based on the almost universally shared premise that when it comes to assets and retirement income, more is always better. But I have gone through this process intimately with hundreds of people, and one thing I've seen time and time again is this: Statistically, there doesn't seem to be a reliable correlation between how much money a retiree has and how happy that retiree is. We have encountered very happy retired clients who take out less than $50,000 a year from their portfolios. And we've seen a few who live on generous six-figure incomes and are quite unhappy.

Ultimately, having large numbers under your name in distant computers won't bring you comfort, serenity, or satisfaction—peace of mind, in other words. No matter how much or how little money you have, you face the same challenge in retirement: to know where you are, to accept where you are, and to focus on the most important priorities in your life, whatever they are. This chapter will show you how to do that.

I have found that when people retire, their financial resources usually fall somewhere along a scale.

At one end of the scale, retirees have income and assets that are barely adequate to meet their needs. These people must manage and use their resources as effectively and productively as possible. Extras must be rationed carefully. Running out of money is a potential threat. At the other end of the scale, I've known people with so much money that their so-called problem was overcoming psychological hurdles that made them uncomfortable spending what they could easily afford. Running out of money seemed like only a remote possibility.

Most of us, of course, fall somewhere in between these extremes. When you retire, you need a withdrawal strategy that's appropriate for where you are on this scale.

If you have barely adequate resources, the challenge is to find a way to cover your basic needs, taking inflation into account, without putting yourself in danger of running out of money. Because investment returns can't be known in advance, this obviously can be difficult. Sometimes I encourage people in this situation to postpone retirement, if they can, in order to build up more savings.

For people with tons of money, the challenge can be to loosen up and use their money in satisfying ways without fear. I often find myself encouraging these retirees to spend more than they want to.

Unfortunately, I believe most retirees pay too little attention to how they will take money out of their portfolios. It can be tempting, after a lifetime of working and saving, to pay yourself whatever retirement salary will make you happy. But unless you know you don't have long to live, that can be a big mistake.

The critical question is how much of a portfolio you can or should tap on an annual basis. In Chapter 5, I suggested a ballpark rule of thumb that you should start retirement with savings equal to 25 times the amount you'll need from your portfolio in your first year of retirement. That implies an annual withdrawal rate of 4 percent.

Most textbooks and many advisers caution against taking out more than 4 percent of a portfolio annually. I'm certainly in favor of conservative financial management, and if everybody could retire without taking out more than 4 percent per year, I'd be all in favor of it. If you can do that, I'm delighted for you.

However, many people don't have enough assets to do that. And quite frankly, I believe the investment results from Your Ideal Portfolio will be better than those of the more standard portfolios assumed by the experts. If this is true, then that superior performance gives retirees a bit more room to spend what they have saved.

With clients and in our workshops, we typically present examples based on annual withdrawals of 4 percent to 6 percent. The lower the withdrawal rate, the less the risk of running out of money. And it's obvious that a lower rate means less income with which to live it up.

Before we get into the specifics, I want to emphasize something about the care and nurturing of a retirement portfolio. No matter how much money you have, you can't necessarily sustain any withdrawal rate from a portfolio that's invested in the wrong assets. That means we must visit asset allocation once again—and this time we'll dig a bit deeper in order to discover something interesting.

As mentioned in Chapter 9 in our discussion of international equity funds, anybody who is regularly withdrawing money from a portfolio must pay attention to more than raw return figures. Although it might not be intuitively obvious, the details of how that return is achieved can make a huge difference to the long-term success of a portfolio that is supporting withdrawals.

When you're relying on your portfolio for withdrawals, you've got to treat that portfolio with tender loving care by protecting it from losses. This is simple mathematics. Even one terrible year can ruin things for a retiree.

Consider a hypothetical retirement scenario that starts with $1 million and a withdrawal strategy of taking out 5 percent ($50,000) the first year and increasing that withdrawal by 3.5 percent every year to keep up with presumed inflation. As the scheduled withdrawals go up relentlessly, they take an increasing bite out of the portfolio. The most important thing we look at in this simulation is not the annualized return of the portfolio. It's the value of the portfolio from year to year. This is the crucial measure of whether a retiree is in any danger of running out of money.

If you invest a lump sum and leave it alone, you probably care most about how much you wind up with eventually; it doesn't matter (at least mathematically) how you get there. If your portfolio lost 50 percent the first year and then enjoyed an unending run of 14 percent annual gains (this is too good to be true in real life, but it makes the point well), you could be happy. In 17 years, you would nearly quadruple your money, even without adding any new investments.

But it might surprise you to know that the very same hypothetical series of returns could spell disaster for a retiree making annual withdrawals of 5 percent. The 14 percent annual returns (after the first year) are very favorable. But when they occur after a 50 percent loss in a $1 million portfolio with gradually increasing withdrawals, they would leave an investor broke after 20 years.

You can see this demonstrated in Table 13.1. Although that example is pure fiction, this sort of thing happens in real life.

Table 13.2 shows year-by-year results of retiring on 6 percent withdrawals as previously described, using real returns from two very

**Table 13.1  Hypothetical Retirement Scenario, $1 Million Portfolio**

| Year | Withdrawal | Return | Ending Value |
|------|-----------|--------|--------------|
| 1 | $50,000 | −50% | $475,000 |
| 2 | $51,750 | 14% | $482,505 |
| 3 | $53,561 | 14% | $488,996 |
| 4 | $55,436 | 14% | $494,258 |
| 5 | $57,376 | 14% | $498,046 |
| 6 | $59,384 | 14% | $500,074 |
| 7 | $61,463 | 14% | $500,017 |
| 8 | $63,614 | 14% | $497,499 |
| 9 | $65,840 | 14% | $492,091 |
| 10 | $68,145 | 14% | $483,299 |
| 11 | $70,530 | 14% | $470,556 |
| 12 | $72,998 | 14% | $453,216 |
| 13 | $75,553 | 14% | $430,535 |
| 14 | $78,198 | 14% | $401,665 |
| 15 | $80,935 | 14% | $365,632 |
| 16 | $83,767 | 14% | $321,326 |
| 17 | $86,699 | 14% | $267,474 |
| 18 | $89,734 | 14% | $202,624 |
| 19 | $92,874 | 14% | $125,115 |
| 20 | $96,125 | 14% | $33,048 |
| 21 | $99,489 | 14% | broke! |

**Table 13.2   Bond Returns versus Stock Returns, 1973–1985, $1 Million Portfolio**

| S&P 500 Index Return | Ending Value | Withdrawal | Year | Bonds Return | Ending Value |
|---|---|---|---|---|---|
| −14.7% | $801,820 | $60,000 | **1973** | 3.3% | $971,020 |
| −26.5% | $543,694 | $62,100 | **1974** | 5.9% | $962,546 |
| 37.2% | $657,765 | $64,274 | **1975** | 9.5% | $983,609 |
| 23.8% | $731,958 | $66,523 | **1976** | 12.3% | $1,029,887 |
| −7.2% | $615,363 | $68,851 | **1977** | 3.3% | $992,750 |
| 6.6% | $580,012 | $71,261 | **1978** | 2.1% | $940,840 |
| 18.4% | $599,408 | $73,755 | **1979** | 6.0% | $919,110 |
| 32.4% | $692,547 | $76,337 | **1980** | 6.4% | $896,711 |
| −4.9% | $583,475 | $79,009 | **1981** | 10.5% | $903,561 |
| 21.4% | $609,065 | $81,774 | **1982** | 26.1% | $1,036,273 |
| 22.5% | $642,425 | $84,636 | **1983** | 8.6% | $1,033,478 |
| 6.3% | $589,781 | $87,598 | **1984** | 14.4% | $1,082,087 |
| 32.2% | $659,833 | $90,664 | **1985** | 18.1% | $1,170,870 |

different asset classes for 1973 through 1985. I didn't choose that period at random. I chose it because during that span of 13 years, the annualized returns of the S&P 500 Index and the Lehman Brothers Intermediate Government/Corporate Bond Index were nearly identical: 9.6 percent for the S&P 500 Index and 9.5 percent for the bond index. For an investor in the accumulation stage and not yet taking withdrawals, each of these indexes in those years would have turned an initial $10,000 lump-sum investment into nearly $33,000.

But for retirees taking increasing withdrawals, the stock returns in those years would have crippled the portfolio. By the end of 1985, the stock portfolio was worth about $660,000, less than seven times the 1986 scheduled withdrawal. Short of miraculous future returns, this portfolio was clearly doomed after only 13 years. The bond portfolio, which had escaped heavy losses in 1973 and 1974, was much healthier.

Out of curiosity, I wondered what would have happened if this simulation had continued for another 20 years, through 2007. That period included one of the great bull markets of the past century, a time when the S&P 500 Index was very productive. Oops! This S&P

500 Index portfolio went broke in 1996, before it could take advantage of the great returns of the late 1990s. From 1973 through 1996, the index had an annualized return of 12.3 percent. This period included 11 calendar years with returns of over 20 percent, six of them over 30 percent. Yet the portfolio simply could not remain solvent.

Table 13.3 shows this continuation through 2003. You'll see that the bond index held up just fine for the first 20 years of this simulation, but by the late 1990s it was clear that the ever-increasing scheduled withdrawals would bring down the portfolio. And indeed, it was broke after 2003.

So here's another important point I want you to take away from this chapter: Simplistic retirement projections that use constant returns, even conservative ones, can't do justice to the damage from losing years. In retirement, it's crucial to find the lowest-risk way to get the return you need. If you keep the risk low enough, you can get along quite nicely with a lower return. That's why a retirement portfolio can almost always benefit from a healthy dose of fixed-income funds. And it's why, as we discussed in Chapter 9, the equity part of a retirement portfolio should include international funds.

Now let's move into another very interesting aspect of distributions. I'd like to start with Table 13.4, which shows two distribution plans using Your Ideal Portfolio with real returns from 1970 through 2007. On the right you'll see the effect of taking out $40,000 the first year and increasing the amount annually by 3.5 percent to cover presumed inflation. On the left is a more aggressive plan based on 6 percent annual withdrawals.

Both these scenarios held up very well, partly because the years covered by this table were quite favorable for long-term investors who diversified properly, and also because the risks of the portfolio were tempered with a 40 percent portion in fixed income.

You might conclude from this that taking 6 percent withdrawals is a no-sweat proposition—and you might decide to take out even more. But the success reflected in Table 13.4 is a delicate balance that can easily be upset. If you calculated these results using distributions starting at $80,000, you would find that the portfolio went broke by 2001. Yet the retiree who withdrew starting at $60,000 a year wound up with a very big portfolio—almost $4.3 million by the end of 1991—and could have afforded to spend quite a bit more than $123,566 that year.

**Table 13.3    Bond Returns versus Stock Returns, 1973–2003, $1 Million Portfolio**

| S&P 500 Index Returns | Ending Value | Withdrawal | Year | Bond Returns | Ending Value |
|---|---|---|---|---|---|
| −14.7% | $801,820 | $60,000 | **1973** | 3.3% | $971,020 |
| −26.5% | $543,694 | $62,100 | **1974** | 5.9% | $962,546 |
| 37.2% | $657,765 | $64,274 | **1975** | 9.5% | $983,609 |
| 23.8% | $731,958 | $66,523 | **1976** | 12.3% | $1,029,887 |
| −7.2% | $615,363 | $68,851 | **1977** | 3.3% | $992,750 |
| 6.6% | $580,012 | $71,261 | **1978** | 2.1% | $940,840 |
| 18.4% | $599,408 | $73,755 | **1979** | 6.0% | $919,110 |
| 32.4% | $692,547 | $76,337 | **1980** | 6.4% | $896,711 |
| −4.9% | $583,475 | $79,009 | **1981** | 10.5% | $903,561 |
| 21.4% | $609,065 | $81,774 | **1982** | 26.1% | $1,036,273 |
| 22.5% | $642,425 | $84,636 | **1983** | 8.6% | $1,033,478 |
| 6.3% | $589,781 | $87,598 | **1984** | 14.4% | $1,082,087 |
| 32.2% | $659,833 | $90,664 | **1985** | 18.1% | $1,170,870 |
| 18.5% | $670,705 | $93,837 | **1986** | 13.1% | $1,218,124 |
| 5.2% | $603,410 | $97,122 | **1987** | 3.7% | $1,162,479 |
| 16.8% | $587,374 | $100,521 | **1988** | 6.7% | $1,133,110 |
| 31.5% | $635,585 | $104,039 | **1989** | 12.7% | $1,159,762 |
| −3.1% | $511,539 | $107,681 | **1990** | 9.2% | $1,148,873 |
| 30.5% | $522,117 | $111,449 | **1991** | 14.6% | $1,188,888 |
| 7.6% | $437,681 | $115,350 | **1992** | 7.2% | $1,150,833 |
| 10.1% | $350,441 | $119,387 | **1993** | 8.8% | $1,122,212 |
| 1.3% | $229,824 | $123,566 | **1994** | −2.2% | $976,676 |
| 37.6% | $140,260 | $127,891 | **1995** | 15.3% | $978,650 |
| 23.0% | **broke!** | $132,367 | **1996** | 4.1% | $880,981 |
| 33.4% | | $137,000 | **1997** | 7.9% | $802,756 |
| 28.6% | | $141,795 | **1998** | 8.4% | $716,482 |
| 21.0% | | $146,758 | **1999** | 0.4% | $572,003 |
| −9.1% | | $151,894 | **2000** | 10.1% | $462,540 |
| −11.9% | | $157,210 | **2001** | 9.0% | $332,809 |
| −22.1% | | $162,713 | **2002** | 9.8% | $186,765 |
| 28.7% | | $168,408 | **2003** | 4.3% | $19,147 |

**Table 13.4    Retiring on $1 Million with Your Ideal Portfolio: Aggressive Fixed versus Conservative Fixed Withdrawals**

| Aggressive Distribution | End of Year Balance | Year | Conservative Distribution | End of Year Balance |
|---|---|---|---|---|
| $60,000 | $964,684 | **1970** | $40,000 | $985,447 |
| $62,100 | $1,082,258 | **1971** | $41,400 | $1,132,285 |
| $64,274 | $1,198,549 | **1972** | $42,849 | $1,283,704 |
| $66,523 | $1,018,886 | **1973** | $44,349 | $1,116,257 |
| $68,851 | $832,624 | **1974** | $45,901 | $938,890 |
| $71,261 | $989,648 | **1975** | $47,507 | $1,159,286 |
| $73,755 | $1,072,005 | **1976** | $49,170 | $1,300,663 |
| $76,337 | $1,161,541 | **1977** | $50,891 | $1,460,560 |
| $79,009 | $1,287,311 | **1978** | $52,672 | $1,676,774 |
| $81,774 | $1,331,382 | **1979** | $54,516 | $1,794,428 |
| $84,636 | $1,474,723 | **1980** | $56,424 | $2,058,713 |
| $87,598 | $1,451,882 | **1981** | $58,399 | $2,097,003 |
| $90,664 | $1,589,989 | **1982** | $60,443 | $2,382,655 |
| $93,837 | $1,812,884 | **1983** | $62,558 | $2,816,948 |
| $97,122 | $1,873,017 | **1984** | $64,748 | $3,010,986 |
| $100,521 | $2,321,477 | **1985** | $67,014 | $3,865,212 |
| $104,039 | $2,794,791 | **1986** | $69,359 | $4,794,174 |
| $107,681 | $3,000,075 | **1987** | $71,787 | $5,282,335 |
| $111,449 | $3,408,734 | **1988** | $74,300 | $6,156,138 |
| $115,350 | $3,912,551 | **1989** | $76,900 | $7,233,318 |
| $119,387 | $3,607,062 | **1990** | $79,592 | $6,812,173 |
| $123,566 | $4,277,017 | **1991** | $82,377 | $8,275,622 |
| $127,891 | $4,359,463 | **1992** | $85,260 | $8,617,317 |
| $132,367 | $5,113,246 | **1993** | $88,245 | $10,331,189 |
| $137,000 | $4,984,332 | **1994** | $91,333 | $10,268,065 |
| $141,795 | $5,618,311 | **1995** | $94,530 | $11,817,775 |
| $146,758 | $5,975,617 | **1996** | $97,838 | $12,811,580 |
| $151,894 | $6,174,182 | **1997** | $101,263 | $13,486,404 |
| $157,210 | $6,350,971 | **1998** | $104,807 | $14,135,297 |
| $162,713 | $6,959,906 | **1999** | $108,475 | $15,787,182 |
| $168,408 | $7,008,946 | **2000** | $112,272 | $16,185,822 |
| $174,302 | $6,978,979 | **2001** | $116,201 | $16,417,821 |
| $180,402 | $6,815,735 | **2002** | $120,268 | $16,347,919 |
| $186,717 | $8,648,695 | **2003** | $124,478 | $21,178,853 |
| $193,252 | $9,823,868 | **2004** | $128,834 | $24,462,616 |
| $200,015 | $10,482,773 | **2005** | $133,344 | $26,502,725 |
| $207,016 | $11,912,810 | **2006** | $138,011 | $30,566,612 |
| $214,262 | $13,335,819 | **2007** | $142,841 | $34,683,470 |

A fixed withdrawal schedule such as those we just looked at, starting with either $40,000 or $60,000, is a sort of financial straight-jacket. It can be very appropriate for retirees who don't have much wiggle room in their budgets. If you must have a certain amount of money each year from your portfolio and you must provide for inflation, then this is one way to do it.

Is there a better way? I think there is.

Whether you're on a relatively tight budget or you have more money than you know what to do with, in retirement you need to find the right balance between security and the freedom to *Live It Up* by spending money you can afford to spend. I think you're most likely to find that balance with a flexible or variable withdrawal schedule based on your actual portfolio performance each year.

A fixed plan and a flexible plan may start with the same amount, say $40,000. What's different is what happens starting in the second year. In a fixed plan like the ones we saw in Table 13.4, withdrawals go up automatically to provide an income cushion to deal with inflation, regardless of what's happening with your investments. The flexible plan requires some wiggle room in your budget because your with-drawals can go up or down, depending on how well your investments are doing.

This approach has the great advantage of imposing an automatic feedback loop, making you cut back a bit when your portfolio is strug-gling and giving you more to spend when your investments have been doing well. If you have limited resources, this discipline can force you to keep your spending in check; if you have plenty of money, it can encourage you to use your resources to enhance your life or the lives of whoever you care about most.

Tables 13.5 and 13.6 show you a glimpse of what I am talking about.

In Table 13.5, we look at the fixed 4 percent distribution schedule from Table 13.4 side by side with a variable schedule based on one simple formula: At the start of each year, you withdraw 4 percent of whatever your portfolio is worth. Just had a good year? You can spend more. Just had a bad year? You tighten your belt. In Table 13.6, we do the same based on 6 percent distributions.

In each case, the portfolio is the same and the returns are the same. The only difference is how much you withdraw from year to year.

As you see in Table 13.5, in the sixth year of retirement (1975), the fixed schedule dictated that you spend $47,507. But the year 1975

**Table 13.5   Retiring on $1 Million with Your Ideal Portfolio: Conservative Fixed vs. Variable Withdrawals**

| Fixed Distribution | End of Year Balance | Year | Variable Distribution | End of Year Balance |
|---|---|---|---|---|
| $40,000 | $985,447 | 1970 | $ 40,000 | $985,447 |
| $41,400 | $1,132,285 | 1971 | $ 39,418 | $1,134,690 |
| $42,849 | $1,283,704 | 1972 | $ 45,388 | $1,283,515 |
| $44,349 | $1,116,257 | 1973 | $ 51,341 | $1,109,724 |
| $45,901 | $938,890 | 1974 | $ 44,389 | $934,498 |
| $47,507 | $1,159,286 | 1975 | $ 37,380 | $1,166,894 |
| $49,170 | $1,300,663 | 1976 | $ 46,676 | $1,312,536 |
| $50,891 | $1,460,560 | 1977 | $ 52,501 | $1,472,540 |
| $52,672 | $1,676,774 | 1978 | $ 58,902 | $1,683,556 |
| $54,516 | $1,794,428 | 1979 | $ 67,342 | $1,787,617 |
| $56,424 | $2,058,713 | 1980 | $ 71,505 | $2,032,622 |
| $58,399 | $2,097,003 | 1981 | $ 81,305 | $2,045,434 |
| $60,443 | $2,382,655 | 1982 | $ 81,817 | $2,297,094 |
| $62,558 | $2,816,948 | 1983 | $ 91,884 | $2,676,579 |
| $64,748 | $3,010,986 | 1984 | $107,063 | $2,809,929 |
| $67,014 | $3,865,212 | 1985 | $112,397 | $3,540,296 |
| $69,359 | $4,794,174 | 1986 | $141,612 | $4,290,920 |
| $71,787 | $5,282,335 | 1987 | $171,637 | $4,605,817 |
| $74,300 | $6,156,138 | 1988 | $184,233 | $5,224,382 |
| $76,900 | $7,233,318 | 1989 | $208,975 | $5,964,880 |
| $79,592 | $6,812,173 | 1990 | $238,595 | $5,450,337 |
| $82,377 | $8,275,622 | 1991 | $218,013 | $6,430,650 |
| $85,260 | $8,617,317 | 1992 | $257,226 | $6,491,954 |
| $88,245 | $10,331,189 | 1993 | $259,678 | $7,544,818 |
| $91,333 | $10,268,065 | 1994 | $301,793 | $7,259,400 |
| $94,530 | $11,817,775 | 1995 | $290,376 | $8,090,873 |
| $97,838 | $12,811,580 | 1996 | $323,635 | $8,487,298 |
| $101,263 | $13,486,404 | 1997 | $339,492 | $8,642,397 |
| $104,807 | $14,135,297 | 1998 | $345,696 | $8,761,317 |
| $108,475 | $15,787,182 | 1999 | $350,453 | $9,463,662 |
| $112,272 | $16,185,822 | 2000 | $378,546 | $9,379,377 |
| $116,201 | $16,417,821 | 2001 | $375,175 | $9,197,368 |
| $120,268 | $16,347,919 | 2002 | $367,895 | $8,854,664 |
| $124,478 | $21,178,853 | 2003 | $354,187 | $11,093,849 |
| $128,834 | $24,462,616 | 2004 | $443,754 | $12,375,053 |
| $133,344 | $26,502,725 | 2005 | $495,002 | $12,939,630 |
| $138,011 | $30,566,612 | 2006 | $517,585 | $14,399,886 |
| $142,841 | $34,683,470 | 2007 | $575,995 | $15,757,259 |

**Table 13.6 Retiring on $1 Million with Your Ideal Portfolio: Aggressive Fixed versus Variable Withdrawals**

| Fixed Distribution | End of Year Balance | Year | Variable Distribution | End of Year Balance |
|---|---|---|---|---|
| $60,000 | $964,684 | **1970** | $60,000 | $964,684 |
| $62,100 | $1,082,258 | **1971** | $57,881 | $1,087,376 |
| $64,274 | $1,198,549 | **1972** | $65,243 | $1,203,425 |
| $66,523 | $1,018,886 | **1973** | $72,206 | $1,018,578 |
| $68,851 | $832,624 | **1974** | $61,115 | $839,214 |
| $71,261 | $989,648 | **1975** | $50,353 | $1,025,729 |
| $73,755 | $1,072,005 | **1976** | $61,544 | $1,128,828 |
| $76,337 | $1,161,541 | **1977** | $67,730 | $1,238,732 |
| $79,009 | $1,287,311 | **1978** | $74,324 | $1,385,448 |
| $81,774 | $1,331,382 | **1979** | $83,127 | $1,438,889 |
| $84,636 | $1,474,723 | **1980** | $86,333 | $1,600,480 |
| $87,598 | $1,451,882 | **1981** | $96,029 | $1,575,534 |
| $90,664 | $1,589,989 | **1982** | $94,532 | $1,730,451 |
| $93,837 | $1,812,884 | **1983** | $103,827 | $1,971,901 |
| $97,122 | $1,873,017 | **1984** | $118,314 | $2,023,711 |
| $100,521 | $2,321,477 | **1985** | $121,423 | $2,492,165 |
| $104,039 | $2,794,791 | **1986** | $149,530 | $2,952,834 |
| $107,681 | $3,000,075 | **1987** | $177,170 | $3,099,362 |
| $111,449 | $3,408,734 | **1988** | $185,962 | $3,437,431 |
| $115,350 | $3,912,551 | **1989** | $206,246 | $3,838,021 |
| $119,387 | $3,607,062 | **1990** | $230,281 | $3,429,875 |
| $123,566 | $4,277,017 | **1991** | $205,793 | $3,957,142 |
| $127,891 | $4,359,463 | **1992** | $237,429 | $3,906,797 |
| $132,367 | $5,113,246 | **1993** | $234,408 | $4,440,304 |
| $137,000 | $4,984,332 | **1994** | $266,418 | $4,178,464 |
| $141,795 | $5,618,311 | **1995** | $250,708 | $4,554,154 |
| $146,758 | $5,975,617 | **1996** | $273,249 | $4,672,167 |
| $151,894 | $6,174,182 | **1997** | $280,330 | $4,652,804 |
| $157,210 | $6,350,971 | **1998** | $279,168 | $4,612,838 |
| $162,713 | $6,959,906 | **1999** | $276,770 | $4,872,701 |
| $168,408 | $7,008,946 | **2000** | $292,362 | $4,722,801 |
| $174,302 | $6,978,979 | **2001** | $283,368 | $4,528,850 |
| $180,402 | $6,815,735 | **2002** | $271,731 | $4,263,436 |
| $186,717 | $8,648,695 | **2003** | $255,806 | $5,222,430 |
| $193,252 | $9,823,868 | **2004** | $313,346 | $5,697,721 |
| $200,015 | $10,482,773 | **2005** | $341,863 | $5,827,841 |
| $207,016 | $11,912,810 | **2006** | $349,670 | $6,344,644 |
| $214,262 | $13,335,819 | **2007** | $380,679 | $6,792,959 |

came on the heels of two very unfavorable stock market years, and the flexible schedule allows you to spend only $37,380. This is an example of appropriate belt tightening. The variable portfolio ends 1975 (a better year) with a slightly higher value than the fixed distribution schedule.

Now compare spending and portfolio values in the 10th year of retirement, 1979. On the fixed plan, you spend $54,516; on the variable plan, you can spend $67,342. The portfolio values are very nearly equal.

You can see in the table that the differences become much more pronounced later in retirement. By the 25th year of retirement, 1994, the retiree on the fixed plan can spend only $91,333, versus $301,793 in the flexible plan. This doesn't seem either fair or reasonable. Surely a retiree with a portfolio worth more than $10 million should be able to spend more than $91,333 in a year.

You can see a similar pattern in Table 13.6. By 1994, the fixed plan, which seemed generous 20 years earlier, seems parsimonious and stingy: It dictates spending only $137,000 while the flexible plan allows $266,418.

Now if you're paying attention to these numbers, you may have just stumbled on something odd and unexpected. In 1994, the variable plan with 4 percent withdrawals allows a retiree to take out $301,793; yet you can take out only $266,418 with the 6 percent variable plan. Isn't the 6 percent plan supposed to let you take out more instead of less? Well, yes and no.

The math is correct. The more conservative 4 percent flexible plan paid out quite a bit less in the early retirement years, and this allowed the portfolio to build up faster. The more aggressive 6 percent flexible plan gave you more spending power in those early years; but its early generosity meant that your portfolio grew more slowly.

The point here is that retirees who live long enough may eventually wind up with more to spend if they spend less early. Less can become more, in other words. But not everybody will live long enough to take advantage of that effect. Because of declining health, those who live into their late eighties and nineties are less likely to be able to take full advantage of additional spending power.

The more conservative 4 percent flexible plan is better suited for early retirees, who might be able to supplement their lower withdrawals with part-time work for a few years. I think the more aggressive 6 percent plan is better suited to people who retire later (and who therefore have fewer retirement years that must be funded) and to retirees who have plenty of money and don't need to be careful about rationing it out.

Choosing from among these plans is also a choice between the relative importance of taking retirement income and leaving money in your estate. If you retired in 1970 with $1 million and lived for 30 years, following the fixed 4 percent plan through 1999, your portfolio would have had about $15.8 million to leave to your estate. If instead you chose the 6 percent flexible plan, your portfolio would have been worth only about $4.9 million.

So again, I pose the question: Is there a better way? And once again, I think there is.

I think retirees who start out cautiously, for example by following a 4 percent flexible plan, should be able to loosen up a bit if their portfolios start growing substantially. So in my workshops I propose a formula called flexible distribution based on year-end balance (YEB). The idea is that once your assets grow substantially, you increase your percentage withdrawal.

Here's how this works, assuming you retire starting with $1 million. You start with a $40,000 withdrawal (4 percent) in the first year. When your portfolio's year-end balance reaches 1.25 times its starting balance (in other words, when it reaches $1.25 million), bump your rate up to 4.5 percent. If the balance were $1.25 million, that's $56,250. Bump your withdrawals to 5 percent when the portfolio is $1.5 million or more, to 5.5 percent when it's $1.75 million or more, and finally to 6 percent when it's $2 million or more.

I'm not including a year-by-year table to show how this plan would have played out. But I can tell you that using this plan with real returns for Your Ideal Portfolio from 1970 onward, you would have reached the 4.5 percent level in 1973 but would have had to pull back to 4 percent for the next three years. In 1977 you could have once again taken out 4.5 percent, and you would have reached 5 percent in 1979. You could have taken out 5.5 percent in 1980 and 6 percent starting in 1981. If you followed this formula religiously, you'd dip back to the 5.5 percent level in 1982 because your portfolio fell $1,658 below the $2 million mark. But after that, you would have earned the 6 percent withdrawal level, and your portfolio would never again have fallen below $2 million.

You can find a table showing the details of how this plan played itself out each year in an article called "Retirement: When Your Portfolio Starts Paying You," online at FundAdvice.com. For our discussion here, I've taken financial snapshots of these five plans at five-year intervals to create Table 13.7.

Table 13.7 shows distributions that would have occurred in the 1st, 5th, 10th, 15th, 20th, 25th, 30th, 35th, and 38th years of retirement. This shows the trade-off between taking more money out early or taking more money out later. The last two lines of the table show, for each withdrawal plan, the total distributions over 38 years and the portfolio's value at the end of 2007. These last two lines do a good job of showing the balancing act between taking money out and leaving money behind when your retirement is concluded. The two right-hand columns, showing the 6 percent flexible plan and the year-end balance plan, show very even balances between cumulative distributions and ultimate portfolio value.

Every one of these portfolios held up just fine for 38 years in this simulation. So why not just take out more money and throw caution to the wind? I think the answer is that these results could have been very different if the year-by-year returns fell in a different pattern.

**Table 13.7    Comparison of Five Withdrawal Plans: 1970–2007**

|  | 4% Fixed | 4% Variable | 6% Fixed | 6% Variable | Year-End Balance |
|---|---|---|---|---|---|
| 1970 | $40,000 | $40,000 | $60,000 | $60,000 | $40,000 |
| 1974 | $45,901 | $44,389 | $68,851 | $61,115 | $44,155 |
| 1979 | $54,516 | $67,342 | $81,774 | $83,127 | $82,856 |
| 1984 | $64,748 | $107,063 | $97,122 | $118,314 | $146,699 |
| 1989 | $76,900 | $208,975 | $115,350 | $206,246 | $256,952 |
| 1994 | $91,333 | $301,793 | $137,000 | $266,418 | $332,917 |
| 1999 | $108,475 | $350,453 | $162,713 | $276,770 | $346,765 |
| 2004 | $128,834 | $443,754 | $193,252 | $313,346 | $393,590 |
| 2007 | $142,841 | $575,995 | $214,262 | $380,679 | $478,775 |
| Cumulative distributions (millions) | $3.1 | $8.2 | $4.6 | $7.0 | $8.4 |
| Portfolio Value 12-31-07 (millions) | $34.7 | $15.8 | $13.3 | $6.8 | $8.5 |

I can pretty confidently promise that future returns won't be the same as the ones from 1970 through 2007. Whether they will be more favorable or less favorable is impossible to know.

One thing I notice in this table is that the year-end balance plan ultimately allowed the highest cumulative withdrawals even though those withdrawals started off at $40,000. An investor who achieved that result, however, paid a very real price: lower withdrawals in the first 10 years of retirement.

Obviously, there are other possible formulas. It's a rare retiree who can figure out a plan like this and then stick to it for 30 or more years without some modification based on circumstances that cannot be foreseen. Your retirement should be based on your own needs and your own circumstances, and it's very possible that none of these plans will be just right for you.

However, this analysis is very interesting and useful in show-ing the potential outcomes of the important choices you make. Personally I think the year-end balance plan has a lot going for it. Some retirees will like this plan, yet will need more than an initial $40,000 withdrawal from a $1 million portfolio. They might con-sider starting with $50,000 (5 percent) and bumping that percent-age up in smaller increments to eventually reach 6 percent. In fact, my wife and I think this will most likely be the right approach for us when we start living off our investments.

There are other rules that can be added to a flexible withdrawal plan. For example you could specify that the withdrawal would never be less than the starting value, in this case either $40,000 or $60,000, in order to assure you of at least a basic income. This would let you meet your basic needs, even if your portfolio suffered a series of bad years. However, it could require you to absorb the effects of inflation while waiting for a recovery.

The danger here is that one rule gets piled on top of another and the plan could become a complex series of reactions to vari-ous unanticipated events. I don't want to encourage retirees to constantly fiddle with a withdrawal system in hopes of extracting short-term advantages. Choosing your withdrawal method is a com-plicated and critical step.

Do it very carefully, if necessary with the help of a good adviser, and then stick to your plan. If you take a moderate approach based on conservative assumptions, you'll stack the odds in your favor for having enough money both to *Live It Up* in retirement and to leave a satisfying legacy behind.

## Beyond the Formulas

Real-life situations almost always require more than formulas that you can find in a book. The emotional and psychological hurdles can be more formidable than the strictly financial ones. Some retirees are very disturbed if they must invade their principal, even though the invasion might be only a minor scratch.

I recall a couple of clients who retired with $1.2 million, which we invested in a combination of equity and fixed-income funds with risk and return characteristics suited to their needs. From this portfolio, they needed only $36,000 a year.

One year they were upset after we sold a little bit of their equity holdings in order to raise the $36,000. To them, that was simply unacceptable because it meant they were "raiding the principal."

Our solution was to put enough of the account into fixed-income funds—in this case it turned out to be $750,000—so that the portfolio could generate the needed income entirely from interest and dividends. The rest of their money remained in equity funds, which went untouched. This wasn't necessarily the most efficient use of this couple's money. But it made them comfortable enough to stick with the plan.

For clients who want psychological insulation between themselves and the market, we sometimes use a three-pronged approach. Each year we start with one full year of the client's desired income in a money market fund, where it can't suffer any losses. The client draws on this money through the year, gradually reducing the balance.

We put a second year's income into a short-term bond fund, where it is relatively stable. The rest of the portfolio goes into whatever mix of equities and fixed-income funds is appropriate for the client.

In theory, at the end of each year we replenish the money market fund from the bond fund, which in turn is replenished from the long-term portfolio. In practice, we don't touch the short-term bond part of the portfolio; instead we move money directly from the long-term investments to the money market fund. This makes the client more comfortable and bolsters the fixed-income part of the overall portfolio.

There are other emotional challenges. One of our clients, an engineer with a frugal lifestyle and strong savings habits, started with a retirement fund of more than $4 million and an annual cost of living of $60,000, a relatively tiny burden for his portfolio. A few years after he retired, his wife was diagnosed with cancer. Although she could function quite well, she feared that her remaining lifetime was limited and expressed a strong desire to travel. But her husband, knowing that travel can be expensive, balked.

*(Continued)*

He was very frightened about running out of money, and his fear was grounded in his past. When he was a child, he and his family experienced the trauma of living through World War II in Germany. After the war, for a time they lived in a garage in South America. Later he arrived in the United States without a penny to his name.

This problem was psychological, not financial. We helped him use affirmations to adopt a new view of the role that money could and should play in his life. After a while he saw that hoarding his assets would not do him or his wife any good. He realized he could easily afford to use some of those assets to be supportive of his wife, and he did. Years later, she was still in remission and they were both happier than if they had continued to be miserly.

Some retirees figure out their own creative solutions. I recall an extremely successful businessman who had grown up in poverty and had become president of a bank in California. Though he was a multimillionaire, he always thought of himself as a very poor person. I knew him as a legendary tightwad. One day I ran into him at a business conference. He told me he and his wife had just returned from a very expensive around-the-world trip. Frankly, I was shocked to hear this, even though I knew they had plenty of money. I was even more surprised when he told me their children had paid for the trip.

He obviously saw the startled look on my face. "No, no, you misunderstand," he quickly said. He explained that he and his wife had always regarded their money as there for security, not for pleasure. They found it painful to think of parting with those precious dollars.

But at some point they realized that after their deaths, their children—who were all doing fine financially on their own—would likely spend that money for pleasure and enjoyment. If the money was eventually going to buy enjoyment, they decided, they wanted some of that enjoyment for themselves. In essence, they had decided to spend part of their children's inheritance, and he was proud to tell me that the children were entirely in favor of that.

To my way of thinking, this is a success story.

# CHAPTER 14

# Hiring an Investment Adviser

*I found the best way to give advice to my children is to find out what they want to do and then advise them to do it.*

—Harry Truman

During the tough days of the bear market in 2000 through 2002, Oppenheimer Funds Inc. did a nationwide survey of several hundred investors with investment assets of at least $25,000. Half the subjects had financial advisers and half reported that they made their own decisions. The responses to one question in particular stood out to me.

Question: Do you believe it's important to have a diversified portfolio? Answers: Of investors with advisers, 94 percent said yes versus only 22 percent for do-it-yourself investors. This survey wasn't scientific, and Oppenheimer of course had an axe to grind. Nevertheless, those answers tell me that advisers apparently are teaching clients about the value of diversification.

One other response indicated that investors with advisers were nearly three times as likely to expect a comfortable retirement as those without advisers. Just what that means is open to interpretation. But there was clearly some correlation between having advisers and feeling confident about the future.

Investing is a complex business with many facets that must be successfully managed in order to assure a successful outcome. More than 40 years of being involved with

Wall Street has shown me over and over that successful investing is too much for most individuals to do on their own. I believe you'll greatly increase your probability of success if you have an adviser. When you look for the right adviser, there's good news and bad news.

The bad news is that every year millions of investors get poor advice. Some of them get fleeced at the hands of brokers who don't have the training, the experience, the knowledge, or the incentives to give investors the help they need. Worse, most of those brokers have conflicts of interest with their clients.

The good news is that the fastest-growing segment of the financial services industry is made up of independent advisers who don't have such conflicts of interest. Investors who are willing to do their homework and who know what to look for can find excellent advisers whose interests match those of their clients.

To avoid conflicts of interest, you must understand compensation. At the heart of compensation is a simple question: Who's paying the adviser? Advisers work for whoever pays them. Whoever writes the check is the employer to whom the adviser owes his loyalty.

The topic of compensation can seem complicated, but there are essentially only two models, and I'm going to state this very bluntly.

On the one hand, an adviser whose compensation comes from an insurance company, a mutual fund company, a brokerage house, or any other financial services company is not working for you. In this model, the adviser is using you as a tool to fulfill the objectives of the financial services company.

On the other hand, an adviser whose compensation comes exclusively from clients is working for those clients. In this model, the adviser is using a financial product as a tool to fulfill *your* objectives.

I assure you that your choice between these two models will have a big impact on the advice that you get.

To maximize the probability of finding the right adviser, seek one who is independent and whose interests are aligned with yours. If you find the right adviser and use him or her well, you are likely to get several results:

- You are likely to make more money.
- You are likely to take on less risk.
- You are likely to have less anxiety about your investments.
- You are more likely to maintain the discipline necessary to be successful.
- You are more likely to reach your financial goals.
- You will have more time and attention to focus on your other priorities.

Most any adviser will meet with you for a free initial session. You can be sure the adviser has identified clear objectives for such a meeting. You should have your own objectives in mind. At the end of this chapter I present 10 worthwhile topics to bring up when you meet an adviser for the first time.

If I did a perfect job writing this book, you wouldn't need to hire a professional adviser. You would know exactly what to do and how to manage your emotions and your risks. At most, you'd need a coach and a cheerleader. But that's a fantasy, and fantasy can be deadly for investors. Investing may seem simple: Buy low, sell high. What else do you need to know? To name a few: Tax implications, asset allocation, and risk analysis are all essential. Yet it is rare that I encounter an investor who understands these things and can properly apply them.

Here's another blunt statement: If you want to do better than most people, you can either acquire the necessary knowledge or you can hire it. I'm convinced that you will have a much higher probability of success if you do the latter. Sometime in your life, you have undoubtedly hired someone to do something for you. Maybe the stakes were high, maybe not. If you hire the wrong person to cut your hair or the wrong person to paint your house, you may be embarrassed and frustrated. But the damage does not last forever, and you can recover.

Good parents aren't casual about choosing somebody to care for young children. They know the stakes are high. Investors should adopt that same attitude when they choose somebody on whom they will rely for financial advice and money management skills. Personally, I enjoy hiring people who are pleasant and nice and who make me feel good when I'm around them. But I know that if I want to get an important job done and the results are very important, nice isn't enough. I want to hire the very best person—and you should, too.

So how do you find the best financial adviser? For starters, don't do what most casual investors do. Don't trust your finances to a broker. Every year investors lose millions of dollars at the hands of people they trust (but shouldn't) to give them financial advice. (We take a look at why that happens later in this chapter.)

The single most important point is to learn how to recognize and avoid conflicts of interest. To do this, you will have to ask questions that you might not want to ask, because they involve how your adviser is paid. Wall Street hopes you won't be keenly interested in the details of compensation. But I hope you will be.

Your adviser is in business to make money; he will have thought long and hard about his own compensation. Any adviser worthy of your business will be happy to discuss compensation with you candidly and openly. If you encounter someone who wants to dodge the topic or gives you vague answers, look elsewhere.

Compensation for financial advice and services comes in three basic forms:

1. Your adviser can be paid on commissions generated when you make transactions. A stockbroker most likely earns a commission when you buy or sell a financial product. An adviser or salesperson gets a commission when you buy a load fund. For an early warning sign of a commission arrangement, look for the name of a big financial services company on the door of an adviser's office.
2. In a fee-only arrangement, you may pay the adviser by the hour, or perhaps a flat fee for specified services. You'll be buying only the adviser's time and expertise.
3. In a different fee-only arrangement, your adviser may be paid a small percentage of your assets periodically. This compensation grows or shrinks along with your assets. If your wealth grows, so does your adviser's pay.

Each form of compensation gives the adviser a particular kind of incentive. You need to know what those incentives are.

When compensation is based on straight commissions, the adviser's incentive is to generate transactions. The more trading you do, the more commissions you generate. Furthermore, the broker or adviser who is paid on commissions has an incentive to encourage you to buy products that pay higher commissions.

Everybody in the financial industry (except, unfortunately, most of the clients) understands that the highest commissions are paid on the products that are hardest to sell. And what products are hardest to sell? Generally those that are most complex and most risky. Result: Many advisers are most enthusiastic about products that investors want the least and need the least. That is a huge conflict of interest.

When compensation involves only fees regardless of where you invest your money, the adviser has no financial incentive to steer you into certain products instead of others. The adviser is working for you, and there's no conflict of interest.

When the adviser is paid based on assets under management, the adviser's incentive is to see your assets grow (and, of course, to persuade you to let him manage more of your assets). This aligns the adviser's interest with yours. I think this is the best way to pay somebody who takes responsibility for your finances.

How do you bring up the subject of compensation when you're interviewing a potential adviser? A great place to start is to simply ask if there will be any actual or potential conflicts of interest. Any

## Should You Pay an Adviser to Manage Your Money?

This is a question I encounter frequently. I'd like to cite some research that may help you understand my answer.

It's been well-known for some time that the average mutual fund investor is likely to get a much lower return in any given period than the return of the funds themselves. This is because investors don't buy when the market is low, don't sell when it's high, and often sell out after periods of decline, when prices are low.

Morningstar Inc. evaluated 199 actively managed mutual funds and their performance from 1989 through 1994. The average total return of the funds in that six-year period was 12 percent. But the average investor in these funds received returns of only 2 percent because of their in-and-out behavior.

*(Continued)*

In other words, investors in actively managed funds actually received only 17 percent of the returns they could have achieved in this period. Keep that 17 percent figure in mind for a moment.

I would expect investors in index funds to be more savvy. So I was quite interested in another study that Morningstar did, tracking returns in all no-load index funds for the 10 years ending December 31, 2005. (Remember, this is a very different period from the six years in the separate study just cited.) The index funds themselves achieved annual returns of 8.7 percent, while the average investor in them earned 7.1 percent.

In other words, investors in these index funds actually received 82 percent of the returns they could have had in this period. Keep that 82 percent figure in mind, too.

Now you're ready for a very interesting statistic about investors in Dimensional Fund Advisors funds, which I described earlier as the best group of funds I know. With only a few limited exceptions, these funds are available only through investment advisers.

Morningstar studied DFA funds for the same 10-year period ending December 31, 2005, and found that on average the funds returned 9.9 percent. The average investor in those funds received 10.8 percent (before the effect of any advisory fees). In other words, DFA fund investors actually received 109 percent of the returns of the funds themselves.

How could this happen? I believe the most likely explanation is that investment advisers encouraged their clients to buy out-of-favor assets they most likely wouldn't have bought on their own, to periodically rebalance and to invest conservatively enough so they could stay the course through difficult times.

Assuming management fees reduced the real return on the DFA funds to 9.8 percent, it still compares very favorably with the 7.1 percent obtained by investors in no-load index funds in exactly the same period.

Moving from no-load index funds to DFA funds provided a 38 percent increase in returns, *after* paying for the services of an adviser. I rest my case!

---

excellent adviser should be pleased that you are savvy enough to ask such a question. If an adviser seems insulted by this question, this is not the right adviser for you.

Here's another good question that you should get in the habit of asking whenever an adviser makes a recommendation: "Why are you recommending this product to me?" Even better, ask for a written answer that addresses the potential return and potential risk as well as the cost (there is always a cost) to you of this particular investment. This single request, if it were regularly made by clients, would avoid billions of dollars worth of grief every year at the hands of advisers who are mostly just looking out for themselves and their sales goals.

I'd like to talk a bit about brokers and tell you why I think you should take a pass on them.

One of the biggest risks facing investors is what I call adviser risk, the possibility that you may lose money because of inappropriate professional advice. Here's a simple recipe that's guaranteed to produce inappropriate advice: Start with a salesperson who's presenting himself as an adviser. Then add inexperience and ignorance. Top it off with a high-pressure conflict of interest.

Brokers would like you to think of them as your friends. They may be friendly and pleasant to deal with, but I hope you won't give in to the temptation to treat a broker as a friend. A real friend doesn't exploit your lack of knowledge and sophistication.

Brokers would like you to think of them as analysts of stocks, funds, managers, and the market. But although they may be good at passing the tests required for licensing and they may be good at sales, most brokers aren't qualified to analyze securities or speak authoritatively about economics.

Ideally, your adviser's job is to solve problems and capture opportunities on your behalf. But that is not what brokers are trained, motivated, and paid to do. A broker's real job is to sell products.

Brokers keep their jobs based entirely on how well they meet sales targets and bring in revenue. If their clients do well or do poorly, that is essentially irrelevant from the perspective of the people who manage, motivate, and evaluate brokers.

You should want your adviser to make sure you understand the risks of investments in advance. But brokers know that sales are generated by optimism and hope, not by worry and caution. (Investors themselves are partly to blame for this. When all the customer seems to want is performance, and when the broker is under pressure to push certain products, why should a broker go out of his way to point out that these products will probably produce less performance than the customer wants?)

In my mind there is no question which choices investors would make if they knew all the facts. Almost without exception, investors would choose funds with minimal fees, commissions, and expenses. But brokers rarely present those choices to their clients. Too often, the broker goes right into an enthusiastic sales pitch for products that the broker believes will be easy to sell.

Most clients have no idea of the pressures their brokers are under to sell. One broker told me in an e-mail: "There are a lot of good, well-meaning brokers at large retail brokerage firms who would like to recommend investments such as the ones you recommend. But they find themselves nearly coerced into recommending the higher-commission products by the management of these firms."

What's always easy to sell is recent hot performance. Rare indeed is the broker who goes to the trouble of persuading clients to have a broad mix of large companies and small companies, growth companies and value companies, U.S. and international companies. In fact, I don't know that I've ever seen a brokerage client whose portfolio is as widely diversified as it should be.

I believe investors deserve the best investment and planning advice available. They are highly unlikely to get it from somebody whose job is to sell them commissioned products.

So far I've given you my opinions and beliefs, based on my experience. Now I want to cite a study by three business professors, two from Harvard and one from the University of Oregon. This study was done by Daniel Bergstresser of Harvard Business School, John M.R. Chalmers of the University of Oregon, and Peter Tufano of Harvard Business School and the National Bureau of Economic Research.

The professors studied a variety of industry data from 1996 through 2004, representing trillions of dollars invested in mutual funds. They compared funds owned by investors who used brokers with funds owned by do-it-yourself investors.

In the end, they couldn't find any evidence that brokers helped investors pick funds that were harder to find or harder to evaluate or funds with either lower costs or higher performance.

On the contrary, the study found that in 2002, investors in funds chosen by brokers collectively paid $8.8 billion in 12b-1 fees plus another $3.6 billion in front-end loads (sales commissions) and $2.8 billion in back-end loads. That's a total of $15 billion in one year in charges the professors said investors could easily avoid. That $15 billion reduced the investors' returns by that amount, the study said.

In addition, the professors found that brokerage customers owned funds with higher operating costs, on average, than do-it-yourself investors.

Were these higher costs offset by higher fund performance? The professors found quite the opposite: Brokers steer investors toward equity and bond funds that deliver "substantially inferior performance" even before considering 12b-1 fees, front-end loads, and back-end loads, they said. The study concluded that this underperformance costs investors who use brokers approximately $9 billion a year.

(For more on this study, see an article by Richard Buck at FundAdvice.com called "The Right Way to Choose and Buy Mutual Funds.")

I leave it to the psychologists to evaluate why so many investors pay unreasonably high costs in order to get inferior products. I hope I have given you the tools necessary so that you can choose the right funds and avoid this trap.

I know there are many brokers who try hard and do their best to do the right thing for clients. But most clients have no way to know which brokers those are. I have been in this business for decades and have lots of good contacts, and even I still do not know any reliable way to identify brokers who are truly worth trusting. Although they are in the financial services industry, I don't believe brokers are in the same business as I am. I have stopped recommending that people go to brokers at all.

## What You Should Get from an Investment Adviser

Professional investment advice goes far beyond recommendations for putting together a portfolio. A good adviser should be able to help you:

- Define your financial needs and turn them into specific, measurable objectives.
- Project your income and savings.
- Project your investment returns.
- Project your future portfolio values.
- Project your cash flow in retirement.
- Determine the most desirable mix of investments to achieve your individual needs.
- Prepare for and deal with the inevitable periods when the market is unfavorable.
- Complete paperwork.

*(Continued)*

- Open custodial accounts if you need or want them.
- Manage investments and regularly review your objectives.
- Research investments to improve your results.
- Manage your money on a full-time basis if that is what you desire.
- Get objective guidance on all financial matters.

Other valuable services an adviser may offer include advice on assets the adviser is not managing, advice to other members of your family, negotiating loans you may make to your children or other family members, and making referrals to other professionals whose services you may need.

In addition, a good adviser can help resolve differences between couples.

An adviser who does all these things well is likely to be among your most important assets.

When you're shopping for a financial adviser, here are the most important things to look for:

- Experience. Thorough training isn't enough. Your adviser should be somebody who has been in the trenches through good times and bad—and who has a successful track record through it all.
- Lots of knowledge about expenses, taxes, diversification, asset allocation, withdrawals, and risk management.
- A commitment to avoid conflicts of interest.
- A commitment to be available whenever you need something.
- Someone who will listen to you and take you seriously when you aren't happy—even if you don't have more business to send his way.

If I didn't have any good connections in the business, here's how I would go about finding the right adviser. My first requirement would be somebody who is independent, without any relationship to a sales manager. My second requirement would be somebody who is compensated only by clients. I'm most likely to find these attributes, along with experience, knowledge, training, and ethics, from a certified public accountant (CPA) who holds the Personal Finance

Specialist (PFS) designation or a certified financial planner (CFP). However, either a CPA or a CFP can have conflicts of interest. So I would avoid any who have aligned themselves with brokers.

I would also look for somebody who has access to Dimensional Fund Advisors' asset-class funds, which I regard as the best mutual funds in the world (see Chapter 12).

If you can identify and interview three or four people who meet those criteria, you'll almost certainly find an excellent adviser. Whatever money you pay such a person will most likely be a good investment.

Finally, I'd like to end this chapter by talking about starting on the right foot when you begin your relationship with an adviser.

Most investment advisers will offer you a free consultation without charge. For them, the consultation is an opportunity to gain your confidence and your trust and make you feel good about doing business with them. For you, it's an opportunity to size up the adviser's business practices and philosophies and determine if they are compatible with yours.

Many casual investors don't go beyond the superficial feel-good aspects of such a meeting. They are happy to postpone or ignore the difficult conversations about fees, costs, conflicts of interest, and so forth. However, by reading this far in my book, you have demonstrated that you're more serious than they are. So I'm going to tell you how to get the most benefit from an initial consultation.

I'll do this by listing 10 topics we often cover with investors who come in to size us up. Any adviser worth your business should be happy to talk to you about these things. You won't be able to cover all of them in one session, of course. But you might be surprised at how much ground you can cover with a good adviser.

These topics are not only a good way to get guidance about important issues. They are also a way for you to test the mettle of the person you're talking to. If the adviser is more interested in talking about products than in covering these issues, you haven't found the best match.

I've chosen these 10 questions because they zero in on the issues that really make a difference to investors, things that can change their lives.

   **1.** What is the approximate rate of return you must have in order to meet your long-term needs? I have always been surprised at how few investors can tell me this figure. Many people have no trouble at all knowing that their investments are—or are not—doing well. But how can they know this if they don't know what they need?

2.  How much risk can you tolerate? Managing risk is one of the most important jobs facing every investor. If you get this right, you'll have smooth sailing. If you get it wrong, you can wind up being an emotional mess and making counterproductive investment decisions. This isn't an easy or simple topic, and we typically spend a lot of time on it with our clients.

3.  How much of your portfolio should be allocated to stock funds and how much to fixed-income? This is the most basic investment issue in putting together a portfolio, and it's a critical part of the work we do with every client. Your answer to this will have an enormous impact on the results you get— and probably also on how you feel about your investments.

4.  How much money will you need in savings when you retire? If you are within 10 years of retirement, this is a very important number for you. It will tell you how much you need to be saving and whether you can afford to stop working. It's not hard to get a ballpark figure, but the closer you get to retirement, the more precise your calculations should be. Any good adviser will know how to figure this out.

5.  How much money should you be saving every year to achieve your goals? A few people may be saving too much, but most people aren't saving enough. An adviser can run the numbers for you from an objective point of view.

6.  If you're retired, how much can you afford to withdraw from your investments each year? When this is figured out properly, you can make a budget that gives you peace of mind. But if you don't understand the variables that go into this, retirement can be an emotional roller coaster ride. Chapter 13 gives an overview of this topic, but an adviser can help you sort through the choices and find the right answer for you.

7.  At what age should you start taking Social Security? Too many people just can't wait to start receiving Social Security checks, and they sign up for the payments starting at 62. This is perfectly legal and sometimes necessary. But it decreases the size of the payments not only to you but also to a surviving

spouse, if you have one. This decision could help you avoid a retirement dominated by penny-pinching. A good adviser can help you navigate through the trade-offs.

8. Can you estimate what your portfolio will be worth at the end of your life? Unless you are on your deathbed, this number cannot be very precise; it must be an estimate. But a ballpark estimate will let you determine what might be available to your heirs.

9. If you have a choice, should you take your pension or roll the proceeds over into an IRA? And if you decide to take the pension, do you know how to choose the best payout option for you and your heirs? Do you know whether to roll over your 401(k) assets or leave them where they are? This is familiar territory for most financial advisers.

10. Do you own any investments you should sell? A financial adviser can review your portfolio, along with your tax situation, and identify assets that may not be right for you.

Discussions like these are very valuable. If you go to an initial consultation armed with these questions plus the knowledge and understanding you have gained from this book, you will be miles ahead of most people who work with a financial adviser.

That, of course, is exactly what I want for you.

# CHAPTER 15

# Your Action Plan

*The person who does things makes many mistakes. But he never makes the biggest mistake of all: doing nothing.*

—Benjamin Franklin

By this point I hope you understand that the most important decision investors must make is their choice of assets. The asset allocation you choose will have more impact on your long-term returns than your timing of sales and purchases. In the long run, your asset allocation will have more impact than your selection of mutual funds.

But neither your timing nor your investment selection is the second most important decision. Your number two decision is every bit as important as asset allocation—and for some investors it's the toughest decision of all: the decision to take action and make a change. Nothing I write can make you change. I'm an educator, not a salesman. It's my job to inform you and convince you and persuade you, but not to manipulate you into doing something, even if I believe it's in your best interests.

Sometimes change is hard because the task looks overwhelming. In this chapter I've tried to break down many of the essential steps you should take into small enough tasks that you can tackle easily. My purpose is to help you when you get stuck because of inertia or any other reason. The list that follows isn't comprehensive.

But if you ever are unsure what to do next, this chapter should give you plenty of tasks to do (or to review if you've already done them).

At the end you will find what I think of as the ultimate (not a word I use lightly, but it applies here) way to get yourself unstuck, no matter what.

I'd like to start with a true story.

In the autumn of 2001, a time that turned out to be about midway through the great bear market at the start of this century, a prospective client came into our office and asked an unusual question: Why hadn't he done what he knew he should do with his investment portfolio?

This man was sophisticated and well informed about financial matters, a professional in his fifties who had managed to accumulate more than $1 million for his retirement. We had met with this investor almost a year earlier and tried to get him to diversify his portfolio, most of which was invested in technology stocks and technology funds. He had attended two workshops that I led and had heard me speak on another occasion. Without any doubt, he knew he needed to make some major changes in his portfolio.

When he returned to our office that fall, he had lost more than 60 percent of the value of his portfolio since the bull market peaked a year and a half earlier, in early 2000. The losses had set him back years in his goal of retiring early. Even as we talked, the market continued to deteriorate.

"Why haven't I done what I know I should do?" he asked. "Why didn't you tell me something that would have motivated me to make this obvious change?" This intelligent, accomplished man was facing the stark reality of the important difference between knowing that you should do something and actually doing it.

He was essentially telling me that I had convinced him that he should have a more diversified portfolio, but that I had not persuaded him to do anything about it. He was right, of course. And he was not alone.

At a workshop two weeks later, I asked for a show of hands. "How many of you have made major changes in your investments in the past year and a half?" About 5 percent of the hands went up. "How many of you wish you had made major changes in your investments?" A majority of hands were raised.

Few of us are immune to the difficulties of doing what we know that we should do. Habit and inertia are formidable forces. I smoked cigarettes for several years when I was young, even though I knew it was bad for my health. Finally quitting at age 30 was easy for me. But I have struggled for many years to try to keep my weight and my diet under control and to maintain a proper exercise program.

I can't push you over whatever psychological hump may keep you from doing what you need to do. But I can offer you a laundry list of individual steps you can take to get from wherever you are to wherever you wish to be. Therefore, without further ado, here are some of the most important tasks that will get your financial affairs in order and clear the decks for that perfect retirement you want.

- Make a balance sheet that lists all your assets and liabilities.
- Review your investments to make sure your overall asset allocation includes all parts of your portfolio.
- Use the Instant X-Ray portfolio analysis tool at Morningstar .com to analyze your investments. Use this to determine your stock overlap, your asset class distribution, and your overall expense level.
- Break down your portfolio by what is in taxable accounts and what's in tax-sheltered ones. Determine the extent to which you have your most tax-efficient holdings in taxable accounts (where they belong) and your least tax-efficient holdings in tax shelters (where they belong).
- Make a written retirement plan, using a notebook or a folder in your computer. Use this to collect portfolio values, questions and topics to discuss with your adviser, an overall description of your estate plan, income and expense projections, and any other investment-related and retirement-related materials you may want at hand. Include a front-page document that notes your desired retirement date and how much money you'll need at that time to meet both your basic target and your live-it-up target.
- Analyze your spending to make sure it is under control.
- Meet with your spouse or partner, if you have one, to discuss your goals and any worries that either of you might have about retirement.

- Hire an adviser, if you don't already have one, using the guidelines in Chapter 14.
- Educate yourself beyond what's in this book, using recommendations in the Appendixes.
- Once every year, reread Chapter 4 to remind yourself of your three biggest adversaries: Wall Street, the media, and your own emotions.
- If you have a spouse or partner, discuss your estate plan with him or her.
- If your will doesn't do what you want, meet with your attorney to write a new one. If you don't have a will and an estate plan, make this your top priority.
- Sell any investments you own that are in the wrong asset classes for your needs.
- Sell any investments you own that make you pay excessive continuing expenses or taxes.
- If you are investing regularly or want to invest regularly, establish automatic investment plans with your mutual funds. If possible, arrange to have this done via automatic transfers from your bank account or through payroll deductions.
- Schedule one day a year when you will rebalance your portfolio to meet your target allocations.
- If you are in or near retirement, review your withdrawal plan with your financial adviser.
- If you find yourself watching CNBC more than one hour a month, use your cable box to block that channel so it can't get to your television.
- Finally, as promised: If you're feeling stuck and all else fails, pick up the phone and schedule a consultation with your adviser. If you have picked the right adviser, one who isn't motivated to sell you products, that adviser can quickly figure out what, if anything, would be the best use of your time and energy at any given moment in your life.

If you take this to heart, you'll never end up in my office asking why I didn't "make" you do the right thing. More likely, you'll be living it up in retirement. And that's exactly what I want!

## Merriman on Doing It Now

Many times investors go to the trouble of figuring out what they should do, only to be stopped by the thought that they should wait for the right time.

A typical comment I hear goes like this: "Okay, Paul, I can see what I should do to properly diversify my portfolio. But because of what's happening in the market these days I think I should wait a bit."

The reason for waiting is usually some variation on "until things settle down" or "until I can see which way this market is going." Sometimes the reasons are legitimate, such as minimizing taxes or early-withdrawal penalties. But quite often, it's just procrastination and worry.

Still, it's common to find yourself in this situation: You have determined that what you are currently doing is not the right thing for you. And you have determined something else that is the right thing for you. And yet it seems like this is the wrong time to make the change.

When you find yourself in that spot, here's a formula that's worthwhile to remember: *It is never the wrong time to do the right thing. But it is always the wrong time to keep doing the wrong thing.*

Henry Kissinger said it another way: "A problem ignored is a crisis invited."

# CHAPTER 16

# My 500-Year Plan

*Diamonds are only lumps of coal that stuck to their jobs for a long time.*

—B.C. Forbes

If you are fortunate enough to have surplus funds left when you complete your life, there is an enormous opportunity to do some things with this leftover money. It's called estate planning.

Attitudes are gradually evolving about the ways people leave money to their heirs, and my own views have changed over the years. I have decided that when I finally must leave this life, I don't want my estate to simply write big checks to my children and grandchildren. I want the financial results of my life's work to amount to more than lump-sum bequests.

Encouraged by the possibilities of the ideal portfolio described in this book, coupled with the variable withdrawal schedules we saw in Chapter 13, I have devised a 500-year plan for my money. Unfortunately, I won't be around to see how it works. But here's the overall plan: I'm going to leave money in a way that will supplement my family's own income and (I hope) will also give them opportunities they wouldn't ever have otherwise. And my estate plan will ultimately provide continuing support to charitable causes that I believe are worthy of this money.

This plan is the result of a great deal of thought and discussion, and I know it's not what most people would want to do. I'm sharing it with you in the hope it will stimulate your own thinking about the legacy that you may want to leave.

In the 1960s, when I first began working with people on their finances, an important priority for many older people was the desire to eventually leave substantial bequests to their children. This was—and remains—a worthy goal. Economists generally believe that trillions of dollars will be left to the next generation over the next 30 years. This massive transfer of wealth will have profound effects, individually and collectively.

Some fundamental things have changed in the past 40 years. The take-it-for-granted confidence of the 1960s has been all but wiped out. Social Security has an unknown future. The high inflation of the 1970s and 1980s mangled many fortunes that were comfortably invested in bonds that most people thought were safe. Retirement pensions, once a staple of old-age expectations and once the responsibility of employers, have gradually been replaced by defined-contribution arrangements such as 401(k) plans and IRAs.

Individuals are now the ones who must make the decisions about their investments. And they are the ones who must accept the risks involved in those decisions. Gradually but irresistibly, corporations—and society—have become somewhat less paternalistic. Perhaps I have done the same. I like to think I have adopted a more enlightened paternalism. As much as I love and treasure my children and grandchildren, I do not want my success in life to relieve them of the responsibility to provide for themselves. In addition, I know that my wish to be generous extends far beyond my family.

My first priority is to see that my wife has adequate resources to live well for the rest of her life. My estate plan provides for that, and we have set aside other investments for our children. She and I have committed together to the rest of the following plan.

My goal for my estate is to leave something akin to a pension fund for each of my children and grandchildren that will provide a growing annual income to them. I want the assets to be protected from as many of the potential threats as possible that they could face after my death. If I left assets outright to my heirs, some or all of those assets could be lost to divorce, lawsuits, poor investment decisions, or creditors—not to mention an heir who might squander this bequest by spending it on short-term high living, only to be left high and dry later. I don't want that.

I have concluded that the best protection against such contingencies is to use trusts. That way, the assets can be invested and still be kept out of reach of most, if not all, financial predators.

Here is my 500-year plan:

My estate will create a charitable remainder trust for each of my four children. The money is to be invested along the lines of Your Ideal Portfolio, with a 60/40 split of equities and fixed-income funds. This portfolio is likely to grow over time, while the fixed-income allocation and wide diversification of equity asset classes should protect against major losses.

Each year, the trustee will tally up the assets in each trust and pay 5 percent of the total to the beneficiary. As we saw in Chapter 13, this combination of diversified investments and modest withdrawals has a high likelihood of not only surviving but also of growing over time. And if the fund grows, so do the annual payments to my children. Assuming taxes and expenses can be kept to a minimum, that growth is likely to be greater than inflation, providing actual growth in real value.

My wife and I each have educational and charitable causes that we care deeply about. At times that we hope will be many years in the future, at the end of the lifetime of each of our children, the assets in the trust for that child will go to the Seattle Foundation. The foundation will invest the money, most likely following a plan similar to the standard 60/40 pension model that we discussed in Chapter 6. Each year, the foundation will pay 5 percent of the money to the charities we have designated.

I chose the Seattle Foundation for this because it gives me a convenient way to donate money to many legitimate tax-exempt organizations at a reasonable cost.

Obviously, charitable causes that I choose today could, sometime in the next 500 years or so, outlive their usefulness or cease to exist. Under the terms of my bequest, the foundation will have the authority (and the duty) to substitute different organizations when appropriate. By using this foundation, I have in effect enlisted a team of people to make smart decisions and ensure that my assets will continue doing what I want them to do, regardless of future developments that I cannot possibly anticipate.

This is a permanent arrangement, and there is no ending time for it. Hence, my 500-year plan could theoretically last much longer than that. It's interesting to speculate on what such a bequest might be worth in 100 or 500 years. Doing so, of course, requires making some assumptions.

I have no idea how much my estate will leave to each of these trusts, but let's assume for example that I am able to leave $1 million for each of my children. (I hope the amount will be larger, but $1 million gives me a convenient way to crunch the numbers.) Assume further that after taxes, expenses, the annual payment, and inflation, the investments in each trust grow by 2.5 percent per year. I believe that's a conservative assumption, and there's a good chance the growth will be greater. But 2.5 percent is a rate that seems reasonably in the ballpark of what's probable.

By adjusting for inflation, I am able to think about the future results of this investment in constant dollars. I don't know now what $1 million will be worth when I die. But because I am adjusting all the numbers after my death for presumed inflation, these future amounts should be comparable to that $1 million.

Here's what that means: If the first annual payment to one of my children is $50,000, a later payment of $75,000 in these projections represents 50 percent more real wealth than the first payment. (If I didn't do this, the numbers over several hundred years would grow to be almost incomprehensible—and hard to believe.) Even with a low growth rate such as 2.5 percent, when you're dealing in hundreds of years, the numbers get pretty big!

In the first year after my death, each one of my surviving children would receive a payment of $50,000. I expect my two older children to outlive me by about 30 years. Twenty-five years after my death, presumably in one of the latter years of their lives, they would each receive $92,697. Since these are real (after inflation) dollars, by that time they will have received a significant raise from this pensionlike trust.

The trusts for all four children will be created at the same time, soon after my death, and each year each of the four will receive equal payments. But two of my daughters will be younger when the payments start. I expect these two younger daughters to survive me by about 50 years. Forty years after my death, under these assumptions, these two daughters would each receive $134,253, and that payment would reach $171,855 by the 50th year after my death.

I think it's unlikely that any of my children will survive me by more than 60 years (though anything is possible, I suppose). At that time, my initial bequests of $4 million into four charitable remainder trusts would be worth about $17.6 million. By then it would be in the hands of the Seattle Foundation, which would make an annual payment to charities of $879,958 (the combined payout from the assets that had been in four trusts).

Project this out to 100 years after my death, and the charitable payment would be $2,362,753, a huge dividend based on the $4 million left in my will. (Remember we are talking about constant dollars, so these numbers, relatively speaking, are real.)

By 122 years after my death, the payout would grow to $4 million. In real terms, that would equal (every year) the entire amount that my estate put into the four trusts in the first place.

Predictably, the numbers keep growing. By 250 years after my death, the annual payout to charities is $96 million. By 500 years, my $4 million of bequests would pay out $25 billion a year—or 6,250 times the amount of wealth I left in these trusts. That's every year! The principal by then would be worth $500 billion. That's a big enough number that I'm content to stop the calculations right there.

Obviously this 500-year plan requires great patience, a commodity that should not pose any problem to me while I'm in the grave. However, it doesn't require extraordinary patience from my survivors, who will begin getting benefits right away.

This plan is my way to provide perpetual income to my heirs. I like to imagine that any heir who gets a check every year from Mom, Dad, Grandma, or Grandpa could easily develop warm, fuzzy feelings of appreciation. I know that sort of appreciation can stretch for generations and span centuries. One of my colleagues is among the owners of a sizeable piece of waterfront recreational property in the Seattle area that was purchased in 1905 by his great-grandfather. He and his many cousins use this place every summer, and they never tire of expressing their appreciation to their great-grandfather for making this available to the family.

My 500-year plan won't provide even close to everything that my children need, and it isn't designed to do that. It's designed to be frosting on the cake. I hope it will let them do things that they might not otherwise be able to do.

Doing this kind of long-range planning is easier than you might think. The two most essential elements are good investments and a trust document. By now you should already know how to make good investments. (And at the end of this chapter I tell you how to get a copy of the trust documents I used.)

The Seattle Foundation referred me to a local law firm that helped put together these charitable remainder trusts without any charge to me. (The law firm, which is retained by the foundation, didn't write my will but provided language for me to take to my own attorney.) I believe that the Vanquard Charitable Endowment Fund could make similar arrangements. One other benefit of this arrangement is that, because the money is destined ultimately to be donated to tax-exempt organizations, my estate will receive a tax credit at my death.

The 500-year plan is for my children. My grandchildren are beneficiaries of another arrangement that I described in an article available at FundAdvice.com called "The Best Investment I Will Ever Make, or How to Turn $10,000 into $20 Million." This started in 1994 when my son, Jeff Merriman-Cohen, became a proud father (and I a proud grandfather). I wanted to do something really extraordinary for my new grandson, Aaron, and I spent a lot of time thinking about it.

I identified five things I wanted my gift to achieve. First, I wanted to make a one-time investment that would give Aaron a comfortable retirement. Second, the money was not to be used for anything before his 65th birthday. Third, there should be no tax liability on the growth and income of the investments. Fourth, at least $20 million should eventually go to charity. Finally, I wanted to do all this with an initial gift of only $10,000.

With help from Jeff and some professional advisers, I found a way to accomplish all five objectives (although I paid legal fees of about $1,000 in addition to the $10,000 gift). Doing this required three things: a trust, a variable annuity, and lots of time. It turned out that Aaron and I could accomplish this together as a grandpa/grandson team. He has the time but not the financial resources. I had the financial resources and the ability to make a plan, but not the long period of time needed to bring it to fruition.

In a nutshell, here's how it worked: I made a one-time gift of $10,000 to an irrevocable trust for Aaron's benefit. His parents, Jeff and Barrie, are the trustees. The money is invested in a no-load variable annuity, where it is compounding on a tax-deferred basis.

Under the terms of the trust, Aaron cannot touch this money until he is 65. That leaves Jeff free to concentrate on long-term investments, which we expect to return 10 to 12 percent a year. Jeff, as trustee, chose to invest all the money in equities—half in U.S. funds, half in international funds.

If these investments can earn 11.3 percent annually, as similar asset combinations have done in the past, the trust portfolio will be worth $10 million in 2059, when Aaron is 65. Not bad for a $10,000 investment!

At that time, Aaron will receive annual payments of 7 percent of the trust's value, with the payments continuing for as long as he lives. That first payment could be for $700,000, which seems like a whopping amount until you remember that its purchasing power will be eroded by inflation. (Assuming inflation of 3 percent, that's the equivalent of about $144,000 in 2008 dollars. That's not enough to make Aaron wealthy, but certainly a very comfortable supplement to whatever he is able to accumulate on his own.)

If Aaron lives another 20 years and if the investments continue to earn 11.3 percent annually while paying out 7 percent every year, the trust should grow to be worth about $23 million by the time of Aaron's death. At the end of his lifetime, the assets in the trust will be given to tax-exempt organizations to be determined by the trustees, who could be Aaron's own children or grandchildren.

I have established similar trusts for my other grandchildren, and at this point everybody is happy about it.

When I put this plan together, a lot of friends and advisers told me I was making a big mistake. They said I was locking money away that Aaron might urgently need before he is 65. Some were incredulous that I would set up a plan under which Aaron, if he died six months after his 65th birthday, would get only half a year of income from the trust. Others criticized this plan for failing to provide for any family that Aaron may leave behind after his death.

Those are all valid criticisms, and I'll respond briefly here. I believe that anybody who won a lottery to be paid out at the rate of $700,000 a year for 20 years would consider himself or herself very fortunate. I have essentially given Aaron that winning lottery ticket, with two benefits that you won't find in any state lottery: The payments last as long as Aaron's life, and they will (presumably) grow over time.

This arrangement gives Aaron an incentive to take care of himself and live a long, healthy life. It lets him start thinking of himself as somebody who will one day have a lot of influence over how a very big chunk of money will be given to charitable causes. This also lets Aaron accumulate his own resources for an early retirement, should he choose it, with the lotto effect kicking in at age 65 to take care of him permanently after that.

Copies of the trust documents are available at FundAdvice.com (do a search for "irrevocable trusts"). You can take them to your own attorney and modify them to suit your situation.

I can't, of course, ever know the ultimate outcome of my estate planning. But I can assure you that these plans have given me an enormous amount of satisfaction, knowing that the financial results of my lifetime of work will continue to benefit my children, my grandchildren, and the world I love for many, many years after I am gone.

# APPENDIX A

# Ten Lessons I Learned from John Bogle

Iowe a great debt to many other authors and teachers who have helped me understand investing. One of my favorites is John Bogle, founder and former chief executive officer of the Vanguard Mutual Fund Group.

I recommend John's *The Little Book of Common Sense Investing* (John Wiley & Sons, 2007) to anybody interested in successful long-term investing through index funds. I quote this book extensively. The book does a great job of teaching simple lessons that are invaluable to any investor who aspires to rise above mediocrity. With permission from John Wiley & Sons, the publisher of that book (and of the one you are reading), I offer 10 lessons here, with quotes from John's great little book.

## Lesson 1

Control what you can. Many investing variables are beyond the control and even the influence of us common investors. But each of us can control, at least to a great extent, how much we pay for somebody to manage our money. Expenses, in other words. And index funds are much less expensive to buy and own than actively managed funds.

Bogle points out that management fees and operating expenses of equity mutual funds average about 1.5 percent of fund assets per year. An initial sales charge of 5 percent adds 0.5 percent annually for funds held 10 years and a full percentage point if the shares are held for only five years.

> But then add a giant additional cost, all the more pernicious by being invisible. I am referring to the hidden cost of portfolio turnover, estimated at a full 1 percent per year. The average fund turns its portfolio over at a rate of about 100 percent per year, meaning that a $5 billion fund buys $5 billion of stocks each year and sells another $5 billion.

The bottom-line cost of owning an equity mutual fund can be 3 to 3.5 percent a year.

## Lesson 2

Actively managed funds shortchange investors by billions of dollars. Bogle demonstrates that from 1980 through 2005, the Standard & Poor's 500 Index averaged 12.5 percent a year. The return on the average mutual fund averaged just 10 percent. The difference was about what one would expect, given lesson one.

> Never forget: Market return, minus cost, equals investor return. . . . Simply put, our fund managers, sitting at the top of the investment food chain, have confiscated an excessive share of the financial market's returns. Fund investors, inevitably at the bottom of the food chain, have been left with too small a share. . . . On first impression that annual gap may not look large. But when compounded over 25 years, it reaches staggering proportions.

## Lesson 3

Taxes have a huge impact.

Bogle says that the high portfolio turnover of actively managed funds subjects their shareholders in taxable accounts

> . . . to an estimated effective annual federal tax of 1.8 percentage points per year (state and local taxes would further balloon the figure), reducing the after-tax annual return to 8.2 percent.

Despite the higher returns that they earned, investors in the index funds were actually subjected to lower taxes—in fact, at 0.6 percentage points, only about one-third of that tax burden . . .

## Lesson 4

Investment returns look very different when they are adjusted for inflation. In real life, inflation cuts deeply into the returns that investors think they have achieved or think they will achieve.

As Bogle puts it, cumulative end-of-the-period figures "are overstated because they are based on 2005 dollars, which have less than half the spending power they enjoyed in 1980. During this period, inflation eroded the real buying power of these returns at an average rate of 3.3 percent per year."

## Lesson 5

Investors rarely get the returns that funds offer, because shareholders put money in and take money out in counterproductive ways.

According to Bogle, a mutual fund's reported return

> . . . does not tell us what return was earned by the average fund investor. And that return turns out to be far lower.
> . . . Money flows into most funds after good performance is achieved, and goes out when bad performance follows. . . .
> Over the past quarter century, it turns out that the average fund investor earned not the 10 percent reported by the average fund but 7.3 percent.

## Lesson 6

Some mutual funds in fact do beat the market. But it's essentially impossible to identify them in advance, when it can make a difference to you. Bogle makes this point in discussing the records of 355 equity funds that were in business in 1970. Two-thirds of them went out of business by 2005.

> . . . 223 of the equity funds of 1970 are gone, mostly the poor performers. Another 60 remain, yet significantly underperformed the S&P 500 Index by more than one percentage point

per year. Together, then, 283 funds—nearly 80 percent of the funds among those original 355—have, one way or another, failed to distinguish themselves. Another 48 funds provided returns within one percentage point, plus or minus, of the return of the S&P 500 Index—market matchers, as it were.

That leaves just 24 mutual funds—only one out of every 14—that outpaced the market by more than one percentage point per year. Let's face it: Those are terrible odds!

## Lesson 7

Salespeople are motivated to sell the funds produced by their own companies. Investors shouldn't be motivated to buy them. Says Bogle:

> In a study prepared for Fidelity Investments covering the 10-year period 1994 to 2003 inclusive, broker-managed funds had the lowest ratings relative to their peers of any group of funds. . . .
>
> The Merrill Lynch funds were 18 percentage points below the fund industry average; the Goldman Sachs and Morgan Stanley funds were nine percentage points below average; and both the Wells Fargo and Smith Barney funds were eight percentage points behind. . . . The brokerage firm and its brokers/financial consultants must sell something every single day. When the firm introduces a new fund, the brokers have to sell it to someone.

## Lesson 8

Not all index funds are created equal.

As Bogle points out, some index funds

> . . . have miniscule expense ratios; others have expense ratios that surpass the bounds of reason. . . . Today, there are some 115 index mutual funds designed to track the Standard & Poor's 500 Index. Astonishingly, more than half of them carry an initial sales load, albeit often concealed by offering "class B" with no front-end load but with an additional heavy annual

fee (used to pay the broker). The wise investor will select only those index funds that are available without sales loads, and those operating at the lowest costs.

## Lesson 9

The bottom line of investing in index funds is very simple.

Bogle points out that index funds' superior returns come from two basic sources:

> (1) the broadest possible diversification, eliminating individual stock risk, style risk, and manager risk, with only market risk remaining; and (2) the tiniest possible costs and minimal taxes. Together, they enable the index fund to provide the gross return earned in the stock market, minus a scintilla of cost.

## Lesson 10

The index fund fan club extends far beyond John Bogle.

John has a "Don't take my word for it" box in every chapter of his book. The two most famous investors of the past 75 years were Benjamin Graham and Warren Buffett. On page 186 of John's book, he quotes Buffett: "A low-cost index fund is the most sensible equity investment for the great majority of investors. My mentor, Ben Graham, took this position many years ago and everything I have seen since convinces me of its truth."

# APPENDIX B

# Resources

John Bogle's *The Little Book of Common Sense Investing* contains everything you need to create a great retirement. But serious students of investing will want to dig further. Here are some suggestions.

## Online Resources

These days, most serious investors use their computers for research, reading, monitoring their portfolios, and sometimes trading. Tens of thousands of investor-oriented web sites compete for your attention. Many of them also compete for your mind and your money, often without deserving either.

When I'm on the Web, here are my favorite investment-related sites:

- *Analyzenow.com* is a great site for any serious amateur or professional financial planner. Its creator, Henry (Bud) Hebeler, a former president of Boeing Aerospace Company, has focused his retirement on helping people understand the realities of saving for retirement, as opposed to the fantasies to which many people cling. Casual visitors may find some of his financial planning tools to be conservative and daunting. But they are extremely thorough and reliable, as you would expect from a former aeronautical engineer.
- *DFAUS.com* is the home page for Dimensional Fund Advisors. Here you'll find out more about this firm's investment philosophy along with a large library of academic articles on passive

asset-class investing. The site also contains several informative videos. Serious investors may find it worthwhile to bookmark the investment glossary on this site.

- *Morningstar.com* offers a huge amount of data and many useful articles covering hundreds of mutual funds. You can learn a great deal by using the site's portfolio analysis tools. Especially useful is the Instant X-Ray tool, which lets you see your whole portfolio's asset allocation at a glance. I don't think Morningstar's Star ratings for funds and stocks are very useful, but this site's data makes it a must-see for fund research.

- *AAII.com,* the site of the American Association of Individual Investors, offers an extensive article library and numerous handy calculators. This organization does a wonderful job of educating investors about retirement and helping them deal with issues ranging from cash flow to beneficiary designations of retirement accounts.

- *Vanguard.com* has good online calculators for addressing such issues as how much you should save for retirement, whether you can afford to retire, what kind of IRA is best for you, and whether you should roll over your company stock or convert your IRA to a Roth. Others tackle questions regarding saving for college.

- *TRowePrice.com* has a wide range of excellent tools for planning retirement, college funding, estate planning, and dealing with taxes. I'm a fan of this company's moderate-to-conservative approach to investing.

- *FundAdvice.com* contains hundreds of articles that I and members of my staff have written over the years. Here's where you'll always find my latest writing as well as access to our radio show, along with dates of upcoming free workshops and other help that my company offers. Additionally, you'll find annual updates of the financial information and suggested portfolios in this book. There's also a unique tool: Explode Loads!, which you can use to find a good no-load alternative to any load fund you may be considering. At FundAdvice.com you can also subscribe to our weekly online newsletter and request e-mail notification about our upcoming radio shows.

I receive a lot of questions from investors, and I reply to some of them in my blog. You'll find it at paulmerriman .blogspot.com.

- *Marketwatch.com* is a popular financial web site where you'll find a wide variety of top-notch authors and advisers with many different points of view. Topic areas include investment planning, tax planning, and personal finance issues.

## Books

In addition to John Bogle's book, which I quoted in Appendix A, I keep the following titles handy for reference, and I often recommend them to investors.

- *The Successful Investor Today* by Larry Swedroe (Truman Talley Books, 2003) does a wonderful job of explaining why investing is challenging—and how to overcome the biggest challenges. Larry is a staunch supporter of using index funds to invest in the asset classes that are most likely to produce fine long-term returns. He also does a fine job of showing how—and why—investors should minimize their expenses.
- *The Four Pillars of Investing* by William Bernstein (McGraw-Hill, 2002) lays out investment history, both pleasant and unpleasant, to illustrate risks and rewards. It's written well enough that it's worth buying for high school and college students who want to learn how to manage money.
- *Fooled by Randomness* by Nassim Taleb (Random House, 2005) nails a topic every investor must understand in order to be successful. The subtitle says it well: "The Hidden Role of Chance in Life and in the Markets." Unfortunately, many lucky investors think they succeed by being smart. This leads them to try to repeat whatever they believe caused their success, often with disappointing results. To the extent that this book helps investors adopt a little more humble attitude, it will make it easier for them to do the things that stack the odds in their favor.
- *Why Smart People Make Big Mistakes—and How to Correct Them,* by Gary Belsky and Thomas Gilovich (Simon & Schuster, 1999), is a great introduction to the field of behavioral economics, the study of why we make the decisions that we do. Most people operate on rules of thumb that too often dictate decisions that instead should be made by applying logic and reason to specific circumstances. You'll learn how your actions are

probably being undermined by aversion to losses, resistance to change, and overconfidence, among other things. This would be an excellent book to give any young person.

- *Your Money and Your Brain* by Jason Zweig. (Simon & Schuster, 2007) is the best book I have read on the psychological challenges of investing.
- *Winning the Loser's Game* by Charles Ellis (McGraw-Hill, 2002) puts forth his contributions to modern portfolio theory in an easy-to-read form. Read this book before you bet much money on the premise that you can beat the market.
- *The Coffeehouse Investor* by Bill Schultheis (Palouse Press, 2005) advocates a relatively simple approach to managing money that leaves time and energy (and money) for nonfinancial aspects of life like mountain climbing, golf, and cooking (to mention three of the author's personal passions).
- *Mutual Funds for Dummies* by Eric Tyson (For Dummies, 2007) is a great primer for people who want more understanding of the basics of mutual funds. If you ever visit my company's office in Seattle, you'll notice this volume on the bookshelves in several offices.
- *The Lazy Person's Guide to Investing* by Paul Farrell (Business Plus, 2006) may give new hope to financially challenged procrastinators who want easy approaches to an admittedly difficult subject area. It's better as a first investing book for young people, to spark their interest in the topic and show them lots of possibilities, than as an ultimate guide for retirees or those nearing retirement.

## Columnists

I don't agree with everything these writers say, but they are always worth my time. I think they'll be worth yours, too:

- Jonathan Clements of the *Wall Street Journal*.
- Jason Zweig, senior writer for *Money* magazine.
- Humberto Cruz, syndicated in multiple newspapers.
- Charles Jaffe, syndicated in multiple newspapers.
- Mark Hulbert at Marketwatch.com and in the *New York Times*.
- Paul Farrell at Marketwatch.com.

# Disclaimer and Legal Information

## Important Disclosure Information

Some of the text, tables, and figures in this book reflect hypothetical performance results. Although the author has done his best to present this information fairly, hypothetical performance is still potentially misleading. Hypothetical data does not represent actual performance and should not be interpreted as an indication of actual performance. Hypothetical data is based on transactions that were not made. Instead, trades were simulated, based on knowledge that was available only after the fact and thus with the benefit of hindsight. Unless otherwise indicated, the results presented in this book do not include any impact of taxes.

The performance results reflect the reinvestment of dividends. Past performance may not be indicative of future results. Therefore, no current or prospective investor should assume that future performance will be profitable, or equal. Neither the previous reflected performance, nor the performance results for any of the comparative benchmarks are provided.

## Data Sources

The following data sources were used to develop the results shown in this book. Many of these returns depend in whole or in part on academic simulations gathered and developed by Dimensional Fund Advisors (DFA). Unless otherwise noted, returns include any applicable interest and dividends and assume annual rebalancing. Monthly rebalancing is assumed in Table 7.3, Table 9.1, Table 9.2., and Table 10.1.

*Equities*

| | |
|---|---|
| CRSP 6-10 Index | Small Cap Index holding stocks in the 6th through 10th decile rankings in market capitalization. |
| Emerging Markets | DFEMX to May 1994, DFA simulation back to Jan. 1987. |
| Emerging Market Small Cap | DEMSX back to 1999, DFA simulation back to Jan. 1987. |
| Emerging Market Value | DFEVX back to 1999, DFA simulation back to Jan. 1987. |
| Emerging Market Core | DFCEX from May 2005. |
| International Large Cap | DFALX back to 1992, MSCI EAFE back to 1970. |
| International Large Cap Value | DFIVX back to Mar 1994, DFA simulation back to 1975. |
| International Small Cap | DFISX back to Oct. 1996, DFA simulation back to 1970. |
| International Small Value | DISVX back to 1995. |
| Large Growth | DFA simulation back to 1927. |
| Large Value | DFLVX back to 1994, DFA simulation back to 1927. |
| Micro Cap (or Small Cap) | DFSCX back to 1983, Dimensional US Micro Cap Index to 1970. |
| Real Estate Investment Trusts | DFREX back to Jan. 1993, Don Keim REIT Index 1975-1992, NAREIT 1972–1974. |
| S&P 500 | January 1990-Present: Standard & Poor's Index Services Group; January 1926-December 1989: Ibbotson data courtesy of © Stocks, Bonds, Bills and Inflation Yearbook™, Ibbotson Associates, (annually updated by Roger C. Ibbotson and Rex A. Sinquefield). |
| Small Value | DFSVX back to 1994, DFA simulation back to 1927. |

## Bonds and Inflation

| | |
|---|---|
| 5-Year T-Notes | Back to 1964. *Stocks, Bonds, Bills, and Inflation 2003 Yearbook,* Ibbotson Associates, Chicago (annually updated); Intermediate Five Year Treasury Notes. |
| Lehman Government Credit Index | 50% long-term corp., 50% long-term government for 1970-1972 (from DFA Matrix 2004), Lehman Bros. Government/Credit Bond Index from 1973 to present. |
| Long-Term Corporate Bonds | Back to 1926. *Stocks, Bonds, Bills, and Inflation 2003 Yearbook,* Ibbotson Associates, Chicago (annually updated); Long-Term Corporate Bonds. |
| Long-Term (20-Year) Government Bonds | Back to 1926. *Stocks, Bonds, Bills, and Inflation 2003 Yearbook,* Ibbotson Associates, Chicago (annually updated); Long-Term Government Bonds. |
| 1-year Treasury Index | Back to 1963, Merrill Lynch GC03 Index |
| Merrill Lynch U.S. 1-3 year Treasuries | Back to July 1977, Merill Lynch G102 Index |
| Lehman Brothers Government Bond Index | Back to Jan. 1973, Lehman Brothers. |
| Lehman U.S. TIPs | Back to March 1997, Morningstar. |
| DFA Intermediate Government Bonds | DFIGX, Morningstar. |
| Vanguard Short-Term Federal | VSGBX, Morningstar. |
| Vanguard Short-Term Treasuries | VFISX, Morningstar. |

| | |
|---|---|
| Vanguard Intermediate-Term Treasuries | VFIIX, Morningstar. |
| Vanguard Inflation Protected Securities | VIPSX, Morningstar. |

### *Portfolios One through Six*

- Short/Intermediate Bond Allocation: 50% in Intermediate-Term Government, 30% in Short-Term Treasuries and 20% in TIPs
- International Allocations: 1970–1974: 50% Int. LC, 50% Int. SC; 1975–1986: 25% Int. LC, 25% Int. LCV, 50% Int. SC; 1987–1994: 20% Int. LC, 20% Int. LCV, 10% EM, 5% EMS, 5% EMV, 40% Int. SC; 1995–2005: 20% Int. LC, 20% Int. LCV, 10% EM, 5% EMS, 5% EMV, 20% Int. SC, 20% Int. SCV; 2006–2007: 20% each in Int. LC, Int. LCV, Int. SC, Int. SCV, and EM Core.

### *Tables 13.3, 13.4, 13.5, 13.6, 13.7*

- Fees are calculated based on Schwab custodial fees, which average around 10 basis points, and the Merriman asset-based fee schedule, imposed yearly.
- Initial Investment is $1,000,000.
- Distribution is at the beginning of each year.

# Index